this is life

A Publication of Tall Pine Books
119 E Center Street, Suite B4A | Warsaw, Indiana 46580
www.tallpinebooks.com

| 1 22 22 20 16 02 |

Published in the United States of America

THIS IS LIFE

A Passionate Pursuit of God's Presence

Aaron and Julie Schilling

CONTENTS

FOREWORD

There is nothing I value more than the presence of God. A life dedicated to the Lord and His will requires God's consistent presence and guidance. I truly believe all that you do needs His voice and wisdom. As a missionary, I have spent the last seven years constantly encountering situations and problems that I personally lacked the ability to solve. I needed His presence to give me wisdom and guidance on a daily basis, even for the simplest things. It was a resounding lesson that no matter where I am in the world or what job I am doing, His presence in my life has to be my focus.

This book will encourage you and give you incredible and practical ways to live with God's presence in your life. I have known Aaron and his wife for over 15 years and have watched him live out his constant search and longing for the presence of God. I have been able to see them raise their children in the same manner; however, it is their longing for others to know His presence that I find truly inspiring. I loved reading this book and found myself both encouraged and challenged. Each chapter has a beautiful mix of biblical study, practical applications, and personal examples.

I truly believe, no matter who you are or where you are in your faith, you will find personal revelation and growth through what you read. I pray that this book blesses you as much as it blessed me and that you will continue to daily seek the beautiful and life-changing presence of the Lord!

–BRI PERRY
Missionary

INTRODUCTION

Over 20 years ago, I had a man that came to me concerned about me and my wife, Julie. He took me aside and began to give me some unsolicited instruction. I listened and was respectful, but he said something that exposed him. He said to me, "You are all about the presence of God, but I am all about prophecy." He didn't say it as a compliment, but I took it as one, because the presence of God is everything to me. The prophetic is nothing without the presence of God. The gifts and fruits of the Spirit are nothing without the presence of God. You cannot separate the Holy Spirit from the presence of God. The Holy Spirit is His presence, and His presence is our life!

Over the years, I have seen people who want the benefits of the presence of God without paying the price. They think that the cost is too great. Others live in fear of the presence of God, thinking to themselves, "what if this happens?" or "what if that happens?" They live in the negative prison of "what if?" What most forget is that the Holy Spirit is a comforter, but there is no comfort for sin. You have to be willing to be made clean to experience the comfort and peace of His presence. You have to understand that whatever the upfront cost is, the reward in God's presence is far greater. I have never regretted one day of my life giving it all for the presence of God!

"We follow the cloud and not the crowd" is a saying I've heard many times and it's one to live by. We follow the presence of God, regardless of where the majority are going. We follow His presence over the opinion of others and what is popular. Sometimes you have to follow God's presence over what you think you want. If God would have showed me where I am today 20 years ago, I wouldn't have believed it and I probably would have said no to the journey, but because I have followed the presence of God, I can say that there is no place I'd rather be. God knows what we need more than we do. My flesh would have said no, but because my spirit said yes, my life is better today than I could have ever imagined. Psalm 119:105 says, "Your word is a lamp to my feet and a light to my path." As His word lights our path, we don't necessarily know every place He will take us. We have to follow His Word and His presence one step at a time. Life with Him is one step of obedience after another.

We have a great example of following the presence of God in the Bible in the life of King David. David loved the presence of God, so much so that the Bible calls him a "man after God's own heart" (1 Samuel 13:14). Toward the beginning of his reign as king, the ark of the covenant, which represented the presence of God, was outside of his grasp. In 2 Samuel 6:5-14 we read that David gathered his men and went to get the ark and bring it to Jerusalem, but he made a grave mistake. He did not consult the word of God regarding how to transport the ark and this cost a man his life. After that incident, David left the ark at the home of a man named Obed-Edom and went back to Jerusalem. Three months later, David received a report that Obed-Edom and his family were greatly blessed because of the presence of the ark. This drove him to seek the word of God and figure out his mistake. When he did, he went and brought the ark back to Jerusalem, dancing before the presence of God on the way. What's interesting about this is that when the ark was removed from Obed-Edom's house, he didn't sit back say, "Well, it has been a good run. We had a tremendous three months, and this should satisfy us for awhile. Let's go back to life as usual." Far from it! Obed-Edom packed his things up and followed the presence of God. He and *sixty-two* of his family members became ministers before the presence of God (1 Chronicles 26:8).

Just as the presence of God became everything to Obed-Edom and his household, we have to come to the point that it's everything to us. We need to have the passion and hunger David had when he brought the ark to Jerusalem. His love for the presence of God was so great that his wife, Michal, despised him for it. She rebuked him and he told her that for God, he would become even more undignified than that (2 Samuel 6:22)! Again, we must follow the cloud and not the crowd. I have decided to be a person who gives it all for the presence of God and I believe if you're reading this, you've made that decision too! In the coming chapters, I'm going to share with you some of the things that I've learned in my walk with God, and my hope is that it will whet your appetite to go deeper into His presence than you've ever been before!

- 1 -
the OPEN DOOR
of GOD'S PRESENCE

What I'm going to share with you in the coming pages is simple but has the potential to change your life. It will help you no matter what you're going through or what stage of life you're in. The truth I'm going to share has the power to propel you into the next thing God has for you, be that a small step forward or the launch you've been waiting for! I can tell you this with confidence because these things changed my life and I know God is no respecter of persons and His word always works!

In life, we often get bogged down by the trials that come. You have to understand, first of all, that there will always be trials you have to walk through in life. Faith in God doesn't ignore reality. However, sometimes things that should be temporary setbacks are allowed to become roadblocks in our lives. We allow things to be prolonged that God has given us the power to overcome.

There are all kinds of things you may be going through. You may have gotten a negative report from a doctor. You may be in physical pain. You may be struggling emotionally, facing rejection or fear. You may be in financial difficulty and the stress is compounding. Regardless of what is coming against you, if you are sitting there and you don't know what to do, I'm talking to you. I've heard people say things like "I'm trying to read my Bible" or "I'm trying to hear God's voice," but nothing seems to be working for them. What I'm about to share with you is so simple and it's going to work! I believe there will be an ignition of faith on the inside of you, as you read this.

Before we begin, I want to talk to you about how I study the Scripture. How many of you remember being a kid and doing a connect-the-dots? You start drawing from one point and make many small connections until the end result is a picture you couldn't see before. This is how I study the word of God, and this is how I want you to think about this, as you read on. We're going to connect some dots! By the end of this book, you will see a completed picture that will expand your capacity, increase your faith, and ignite your hope!

I have done a couple test trials, so to speak, with what I'm about to share with you. The first person had been struggling with racing thoughts for two or three weeks. It was like they had adrenaline constantly flooding their brain. They were struggling to sit down and read the Bible, pray, or even grab a thought. I began to share with them what I'm about to share with you and God spoke! Within a few hours, their brain had calmed down and peace had come.

The second time, I taught what I'm about to share with you to a group of children. My wife and I were the children's pastors at our church and one Sunday morning, I told them that some of them would be marked for life by the encounter they were about to have. God showed up and moved in a mighty way. He began to touch the children in a way that some of them had never experienced and in a way that we had never seen, in the 1 ½ years we'd been their pastors.

I tell you those stories because I want you to know that this really does work! What I'm about to share with you will absolutely change your life if you receive it by faith and apply it. It worked in my life! I didn't need anything special. I wasn't going through a trial or facing a struggle, but these principles that God gave me absolutely enriched my relationship with Him!

To begin, let's look at Exodus 33:7-11,14 which says,

"Now Moses used to take the tent and pitch it outside the camp, far off from the camp, and he called it the tent of meeting. And everyone who sought the LORD would go out to the tent of meeting, which was outside the camp. Whenever Moses went out to the tent, all the people would rise up, and each would stand at his tent door, and watch Moses until he had gone into the tent. When Moses entered the tent, the pillar of cloud would descend and stand at the entrance of the tent, and the LORD would speak with Moses. And when all the people saw the pillar of cloud standing at the entrance of the tent, all the people would rise up and worship, each at his tent door. Thus, the LORD used to speak to Moses, face to face, as a man speaks to his friend. When Moses turned again into the camp, his assistant Joshua the son of Nun, a young man, would not depart from the tent."

The Scripture paints us a picture in this story. Moses would put the tent of meeting outside of the Israelite camp and it was there that Moses would sit and judge. When he entered the tent, the presence of God would come down in the form of a pillar of a cloud, in front of the door. It was here that God would speak to Moses, *face to face, as a man speaks to a friend.*

Now let's look at another Scripture about a door. John 10:1-10 says,

'Truly, truly, I say to you, he who does not enter the sheepfold by the door but climbs in by another way, that man is a thief and a robber. But He who enters by the door is the shepherd of the sheep. To Him the gatekeeper opens. The sheep hear His voice, and He calls His own sheep by name and leads them out. When He has brought out all His own, He goes before them, and the sheep follow Him, for they know His voice. A stranger they will not follow, but they will flee from him, for they do not know the voice of strangers. This figure of speech Jesus used with them, but they did not understand what He was saying to them. So, Jesus again said to them, "Truly, truly, I say to you, I am the door of the sheep. All who came before me are thieves and robbers, but the sheep did not listen to them. I am the door. If anyone enters by me, he will be saved and will go in and out and find pasture. The thief comes only to steal and kill and destroy. I came that they may have life and have it abundantly."'

In this Scripture, Jesus called *Himself* the door. The picture He gave us is of a fenced area, where the sheep were located. There was only one way to enter the sheep's paddock, and it was through the door. Anyone who entered by any other way came to rob and destroy. Jesus told us here that He is the shepherd, but that there is a doorkeeper that opens the gate and lets Him into the pasture. You must understand that the doorkeeper is *you!* Before you ever accept Jesus Christ as your Lord and Savior, and join the sheepfold, you have a door that is closed to Him. At the point that you realize your need for a savior and say *yes* to Jesus Christ, inviting Him in, He takes that door and rips it off of its hinges. He then replaces that door with Himself. You, though, are the one that has to stand in that doorway and protect it. What you're supposed to be doing, as the doorkeeper, is ensuring that nothing comes through the door that shouldn't be there.

The Bible tells us that we are to take every thought captive to obey Christ (2 Corinthians 10:5). Have you ever thought about the significance of that responsibility? A recent study found that the human brain has over 6,000 different thoughts a day[1]. You have the capacity to decide what you do with every, single one of those thoughts. You can look at each of those thoughts and turn to the door, which is Jesus Christ. He will point out which thoughts are going to cause damage and which ones are going to help you. This is how you take every thought captive. You get rid of the ones that are harmful and dwell on the ones that will empower and enrich you. Dispose of the lies and grab ahold of the truth!

Things happen, though. You may be standing at the doorway, standing before Jesus Christ, and all of the sudden, something tries to enter in, just like the robber tries to jump the fence to enter the sheepfold. Harmful things will try to come in the back door! You may be standing in your doorway relaxed, because things are going well, when suddenly, you realize that something has gotten into your pasture. You know they didn't come in through the door, but they are there, nevertheless. Jesus will always tell you if something is there that will harm you. He's a shepherd and a protector. If you realize something harmful has been allowed in, what do you do? First of all, you need to realize that you can immediately evict anything not supposed to be there. You have dominion! God gave Adam and Eve dominion, and they threw it away. Noah was given dominion after the ark came to rest. Jesus said, "all power and authority have been given to me" (Matthew 28:18) and He then gave that authority to His church. You've been given authority as a believer to look at anything that is not supposed to be in your pasture and command it to go in Jesus' name! The Bible says to resist the devil, and he will flee from you (James 4:7)! This is not a matter of pride, but of dominion. If you don't want something to remain in your life, then you have the God-given authority to stand up and evict it.

Sometimes though, the situation won't go exactly like that. Often in a robbery, one person will break in and then go unlock the back door, so that all of his accomplices can get in, with easy access. This happens in our lives, too! Our mouths, our ears, and our eyes can allow one small thing into our hearts and minds, without us realizing the significance of what's happening. If you don't understand the power of your words, then what you say will become a roadblock in your life. Jesus said He only said what He heard the Father saying and did what He saw the Father doing (John 5:19-20)! It should be the same in our lives. We've all said things without consulting with Jesus. We've all watched things we shouldn't have without consulting with Jesus. We've all listened to things without consulting with Jesus. We've all said wrong things or made poor decisions. As the doorkeeper of our life, though, this can let things in that seem ever so small and harmless. However, that seemingly harmless thing can go in and unlock the back door, letting in something far worse! All of the sudden, you realize there's something in your house you didn't mean to let in and the authority you'd been exercising as the doorkeeper seems to stop working.

I've had many people come to me and say they're having trouble hearing the voice of God, but I promise you it's not hard to hear His voice. So, what do you do if you've opened up the door and let something in that shouldn't be in your domain? What do you do if you feel disjointed, disconnected, or out of alignment? What do you do if you feel like an emotional rollercoaster, up one day and down the next? The answer is much simpler than you may think! See, the Holy Spirit always moves in a straight line, and all you have to do is get back into alignment with Him. You don't need a life overhaul! You just need an adjustment. If your back is out of alignment and you go to chiropractor, he doesn't break your spine to put it back together. He adjusts it until everything is lined up the way it's supposed to be!

Moses went into the tent of meeting and the presence of God came down in a pillar of cloud at the door of tent, and *God spoke.* If you are struggling to hear the voice of God, then invite His presence, because His presence is never disconnected from His voice. The presence of God *is* the voice of God. When you feel like you're in a place that you cannot hear God's voice, simply invite His presence to come down at the door of your house and then begin to do what it takes to bring things into alignment! You may need to repent. You may have said, watched, or done something that you shouldn't have done, but when you repent, His presence will *always* bring things back into alignment. I can give you an example for my own life. Everything was going well, when all of a sudden, I began to struggle with something that I had not struggled with in a very long time. I went before God and said "What on earth is going on? I don't struggle with this!" He showed me immediately that I had gone into a store that I should never have gone into. It wasn't about the store itself, but by going in there I was trying to do something in my own strength that caused me to come out of alignment. There was discord and disunity in me, but as soon as I repented, He brought everything back into alignment. You may need to repent for something simple! It may feel like you have a huge problem, but the answer could be something very simple. Listen, mistakes have consequences, and we should all do our best to avoid them, but if you've made a mistake, you can repent right now. Just say, "God, I'm sorry" and ask Him to bring you into alignment and He will. With that being said, you may not even have a problem. Maybe things are going great for you, but

I'm telling you, if you invite His presence to come at the doorway of your life, it'll change you! There is *always* more!

I encourage you to pray this out loud:

"Father, right now, I invite your presence to come down at the doorway of my life. I ask you to bring alignment to everything in my life that is out of joint."

He will answer that prayer right now. Wherever you are, the presence of God will begin to fill that place, even as you read these words. When you invite His presence, He comes. It's tangible. His presence is something you can feel, and it carries His voice. The presence of God is the voice of God. It will bring things into alignment. If all of the instruments in a symphony played their notes in different keys, it would be an absolute disaster. All of the instruments to make something beautiful are there, but the sound coming forth isn't music. It would be an overwhelmingly loud, chaotic sound that means nothing. This is why the conductor uses a tuning fork. When God comes in, it works just the same way! Everything is brought into alignment by the tuning fork of His presence. Every instrument begins to make the right sound and peace comes. Just begin to ask Him to tune you to His presence and receive rest. He will come and speak! Things that you may have struggled with for years will end. Things you've not been able to see will begin to come into focus, as blinders are taken off. Wherever you are, as you read this, His presence will meet you. It's so simple. This is what God longs for His children to do. Life with Him is all about intimacy. He wants to spend time with you, but *you* are the doorkeeper. Welcome His presence and watch everything that is out of joint come into divine alignment!

- 2 -

ACCEPTANCE and REJECTION of GOD'S PRESENCE

As the doorkeeper of our lives, we have the authority to invite God's presence. However, I would be remiss if I told you that there is no danger in seeking after the presence of God. There is danger, but only if you receive and then reject His presence, which is why I'm going to share with you several reasons it is important to stay in the presence of God.

To begin, I want to talk about what happens when someone rejects the presence of God. In this book, we're going look at two different times that the presence of God was rejected. In Jonah 1:1-3, it says:

> *"Now the word of the LORD came to Jonah the son of Amittai, saying, "Arise, go to Nineveh, that great city, and call out against it, for their evil has come up before me." But Jonah rose to flee to Tarshish from the presence of the LORD."*

The word that Jonah received was God's presence, because His voice is His presence. However, Jonah chose to *flee* from that presence, by getting on boat heading for the city of Tarshish, which was in the opposite direction of Nineveh. Jonah was on a boat full of pagans—worshippers of foreign Gods—but he was even more cursed in that moment than they were. They ended up caught in a mighty storm, so powerful that the men on the boat knew it had to be supernatural. They began to cry out to their gods, trying to figure out what the problem was. If you don't know the story, it's a short book and worth reading! Jonah knew what was going on and when he revealed who he was and why they were in that storm, the men on the boat threw him overboard. Immediately, the storm ceased, and Jonah was swallowed by what the Bible calls "a great fish." While in the fish, Jonah repented, and God spoke to the fish to spit him up on dry land. At this point, Jonah is given an incredible opportunity—a second chance. Jonah 3:1-3 says,

> "Then the word of the LORD came to Jonah the second time, saying, "Arise, go to Nineveh, that great city, and call out against it the message that I tell you. So, Jonah arose and went to Nineveh, according to the word of the LORD."

This time Jonah obeyed. The Bible says that when he got to Nineveh, it took him three days to walk from one side of the city to the other. For the entirety of the three days, the Bible says that Jonah declared only four words. In the English, it translates to more, but in the Hebrew, it translates to "forty days, Nineveh destroyed." It was only four small words, but he carried the presence and the authority of God. When the king of Nineveh heard the prophet's message, he declared a fast saying, "Let everyone turn from his evil way and from the violence that is in his hands. Who knows?

God may turn and relent and turn from his fierce anger, so that we may not perish" (Jonah 3:8-9). That king was right and as a result Jonah's obedience, their repentance, and God's mercy, Nineveh was saved. Can you see the contrast here? Jonah went from being so cursed that pagans threw him off their ship to being so full of God's presence that he saw an entire city saved in only three days, simply by choosing to accept the presence of the Lord.

Jonah had clearly been exposed to the presence of God a number of times. He was comfortable with it. He was so familiar with it, in fact, that he knew that if he wanted to disobey God, he would have to escape His presence. He actually tried to run from God. Jonah clearly had a misunderstanding, because there's nowhere that he could have gone where God couldn't have found him. Psalm 139:7-10 says:

"Where shall I go from your Spirit?
Or where shall I flee from your presence?
If I ascend to heaven, you are there!
If I make my bed in Sheol, you are there!
If I take the wings of the morning
and dwell in the uttermost parts of the sea,
even there your hand shall lead me,
and your right hand shall hold me."

He tried to escape to the depths of hell, but even there, God found him! The story of Jonah is one of triumph and failure. It ends with the salvation of Nineveh, which was the intention of God, but Jonah never actually *gets* it. He remains frustrated with God for saving a people he didn't want saved. What's so interesting about the story is that we don't really know why he hated the people of Nineveh so much. Was it just that he only loved the people of Israel and hated everyone else? Was it the fact that, even as a prophet, he didn't understand conditional prophecy? In every prophecy there is a choice and there is always a chance to repent. There is *always* redemptive hope.

Now let's look at someone else in the Scripture that rejected the presence of God. Numbers 20:2-5 says,

"Now there was no water for the congregation. And they assembled themselves together against Moses and against Aaron. And the people quarreled with Moses and said, "Would that we had perished when our brothers perished before the LORD! Why have you brought the assembly of the LORD into this wilderness, that we should die here, both we and our cattle? And why have you made us come up out of Egypt to bring us to this evil place?"

Does this sound as crazy to you as it does to me? These people were brought out of *slavery*, and they were complaining about it. Have you ever heard people like this? These are the people that are constantly looking back, talking about what they had before they got saved. They may talk about money, jobs, cars, or houses. They may talk about what they "gave up" to serve God. Let me tell you something: No person serves God at a loss. God is never going to take you down. Abraham started with nothing and became the father of many nations. If your life has gone downhill since you started serving God, then something is wrong. It is impossible for you to yoke yourself to the God of the universe, the God who abounds in steadfast love, mercy, goodness, and generosity, and not be lifted up. 1 Samuel 2:8 says,

"He raises up the poor from the dust; He lifts the needy from the ash heap, to make them sit with princes and inherit a seat of honor."

THIS IS LIFE
17

God loves to lift up the needy! Even if you do have to give something up to serve Him, you have the promise that God will give you something better! Moses listened to this complaining and grumbling, as he often had to. I have just got to say that as a parent of four kids, there is nothing that irritates my wife and I more than listening to our children grumble. I can only imagine how irritated Moses must have been and how often he must have had to fight anger and frustration, at their constant complaining. He and Aaron had been in the presence of the people and there was an atmosphere of grumbling and complaining that they had been immersed in. They were bombarded by the negativity of the people, and we see in Numbers 20:5-6 that they withdrew from it. It says,

"Moses and Aaron went from the presence of the assembly to the entrance of the tent of meeting and fell on their faces. And the glory of the LORD appeared to them..."

They chose to leave the presence of the grumbling and go into a different one. They went to the entrance of the tent of meeting and the presence of God, His Glory, appeared to them, and *then God spoke*. Out of His presence came His word, as we see time and time again in the Scripture.

You have to understand that sometimes there will be things you have to walk away from. If you constantly allow yourself to be bombarded by negativity, you're going to be in trouble! You have to stop listening to it. You may have to stop reading certain things. You may have to turn the TV off. You need to get into the presence of God and hear what God is saying! The story goes on in Numbers 20:7-8:

"...and the LORD spoke to Moses, "Take the staff, and assemble the congregation, you, and Aaron your brother, and tell the rock before their eyes to yield its water. So, you shall bring water out of the rock for them and give drink to the congregation and their cattle."

God gave instructions to Moses and then sent him back into the assembly! Now, you need to understand that Moses had an attachment to that staff. Sometimes, God will give you something meant to direct you that you then become attached to in a way He did not intend. We see this in the story of the snakes and the bronze serpent in Numbers 21. There were serpents that were killing the Israelites and the people were told *by God* to fashion a bronze serpent and lift it up. Anyone that looked at that bronze serpent was healed. However, they became attached to the bronze serpent, instead of realizing it was just a tool that God used. The Scripture tells us that it became an idol that they were still worshipping hundreds of years later (2 Kings 18:4).

Before we see how this story in Numbers 20 plays out, I want to look at another story in Exodus 17:5-6, which is the first recorded account of the Israelites complaining that they didn't have water.

"And the LORD said to Moses, "Pass on before the people, taking with you some of the elders of Israel, and take in your hand the staff with which you struck the Nile, and go. Behold, I will stand before you there on the rock at Horeb, and you shall strike the rock, and water shall come out of it, and the people will drink." And Moses did so, in the sight of the elders of Israel."

So, the first time God brought water from a rock, the LORD told Moses to strike the rock to bring water for the people. In this second instance though recorded in Numbers 20, the Lord didn't tell him to strike it. He told him to *speak to it.* God spoke to him from His very presence, clearly telling him to speak to the rock and not to strike it, but the story unfolds differently than it did in Exodus 17. Moses stepped out of the tent of meeting, out of God's presence and back into the negative presence of the people. Numbers 20:10-11 goes on,

> *'Then Moses said to them, "Hear now, you rebels: shall we bring water for you out of this rock?" And Moses lifted up His hand and struck the rock with His staff twice, and water came out abundantly, and the congregation drank, and their livestock.'*

Instead of speaking to the rock, as God commanded, he struck the rock in anger. Just like Jonah, Moses set aside the presence of God and because he did that, he was *never* allowed to enter the promised land. Water still flowed from the rock, but there were consequences for his disobedience. There will always be consequences if you set aside the presence of God. Do not just think you can do whatever you want! The old timers lived with a mentality that said, "what must I do to be saved?" but today's Christians say, "what can I get away with and still be saved?'" It is a very dangerous thing to set aside the presence of God and do things your own way.

Now I don't want to get into too much speculation, because there is no end to that, but have you ever wondered why Moses struck the rock twice? Is it possible that God spoke to him again after the first strike, reminding him of what He told him? Let's think about Moses for a moment. In Exodus 3:10, when God called Moses at the burning bush, He said, "Come, I will send you to Pharaoh that you may bring my people, the children of Israel, out of Egypt." In Exodus 4:10 Moses gives God his final of many excuses, saying "Oh, my Lord, I am not eloquent, either in the past or since you have spoken to your servant, but I am slow of speech and of tongue." His focus was on his own inability, but God met him time and time again. Is it possible this factored into his disobedience at the rock? Is it possible that in the back of his mind, Moses was still not sure if his speech was strong enough, even after everything God had done for him and through him? Even after all the times he'd been in the presence of God, the pillar by day and the fire by night, Mount Sinai, and the tent of meeting, Moses still set aside the presence of God in the assembly. We don't know exactly why, from the Scripture, but there were consequences! We *must* stay in the presence of God.

Now, you may be thinking "Okay, but how does that apply to me?" Well, I'm going to show you. When you don't know what else to do, invite the presence of God! That's what He desires. He wants to spend time with you. Especially when you feel distracted and overwhelmed, make time to spend in His presence. I guarantee you'll get more done after you give Him that time than you would if you hadn't. You'll have clarity of mind that you wouldn't have had! God always takes the sacrifice we give and blesses it. Time is nothing to God. He's outside of time! However, when we give Him our time, which is precious to us, He blesses it! Our lives can get really loud and distracting. Without meaning to, we sometimes live with an attitude of "I'll get to you later, God," but that's no different than setting His presence aside. If you know that God's presence is going to come when you take the time to meet with Him, then by not spending time with Him, you are choosing to place no value on that. You're disregarding it! By your actions, you're prioritizing something over God's presence and telling God He's not as important as whatever it is you need to do.

God's entire purpose is to bring us back to the intimacy of the garden. I want to give you a word picture that will help make this more applicable for you. Paul talked about this in 1 Corinthians 10:4-5, saying "and all drank the same spiritual drink. For they drank from the spiritual Rock that followed them, and the Rock was Christ." Now think about this. Christ was beaten on the cross and died for us. As believers, we can either live at the foot of the cross or in the shadow of the cross. The first thing you need to understand is that your life is never going to get worse when you serve God. It only gets better. I'll never understand people who complain about the Christian lifestyle. There's something wrong if things get worse for you serving God. I'm not talking about things that happen in life; I'm talking about the relationship. The longer I serve Him, the sweeter it gets. No matter what though, it all starts at the foot of the cross. It's there that you enter the Kingdom of God. If you've never come to the foot of the cross, and your life is going crazy, you can come, right now!

Pray this simple prayer, before I go on:

"Lord Jesus, I thank you for what you've done for me on the cross. Father, I thank you that you sent Him. I believe that you died for my sins, that your rose from the grave, and that you're alive forevermore. Forgive me for all of the sins I've committed. Come live in my heart and I will serve you the rest of my days."

If you prayed that simple prayer, then I believe you have passed from the foot of the cross into its shadow. As believers, we aren't supposed to constantly live at the foot of the cross, but in its shadow, in constant relationship with God. We see a picture of this in the story of Jesus washing His disciples' feet in John 13:6-10:

"He came to Simon Peter, who said to Him, "Lord, do you wash my feet?" Jesus answered him, "What I am doing you do not understand now, but afterward you will understand." Peter said to Him, "You shall never wash my feet." Jesus answered him, "If I do not wash you, you have no share with me." Simon Peter said to Him, "Lord, not my feet only but also my hands and my head!" Jesus said to him, "The one who has bathed does not need to wash, except for his feet, but is completely clean."

This is what it means to be in constant relationship with God and to "keep short accounts" with Him. Jesus explained to Peter that someone who has already been washed doesn't need to be washed again. They just need their feet cleaned. Sometimes as we're walking in life, we step in something and get our feet dirty. If you're out walking and you step in dog droppings, you're going to act very quickly to get that off. You'll start scraping your foot across the ground and stomping your feet. That's the same way it should be when you're serving God! Listen, mistakes have consequences. There's no excuse for saying things like "everybody makes mistake" and "we sin every day." That kind of mentality will destroy you! It feeds the mindset that you can keep doing the things you shouldn't be doing. With that being said, if you make a mistake or something comes up, deal with it quickly, just like the dog droppings! Walking with God is about relationship. Keeping short accounts with God means letting nothing come between you and keep going on! When you let things linger and you don't wash your feet, you start to slow down or move backward. You may have months go by with things going wrong before you realize what's happened. Far too often, even if we've known the truth, condemnation, shame, and guilt begin to come back in. When that happens, the response is often to leave the presence of God and go back out to the foot of the cross, but no born-again believer should find themselves there again. You can't live that way, but if you do find yourself there, don't despair. You just need to let Jesus wash your feet. Instead, so often, when we make a mistake or something comes up, we go back out to the foot of the cross to get things right with God, when all we need to do is talk with Him. You're in a relationship with Him. Repent and do what you need to do. Talk to Him! Don't go back out into the land of the dead. You're in the land of the living and getting into a cycle of crossing back over into the land of the dead and then the land of the living will be toxic. People go back out, come back in, go back out, and come back in, until something pulls them back out into the world. The reason people don't continue on in the faith is because they don't know it's about relationship. They'll feel the presence of God come into a place and they'll know it's sweet and then all of the sudden, in the midst of that encounter, the devil will knock on their door saying, "Remember when you used to do drugs?" or "Remember when you were violent?" Accusations start assailing them and weighing them down when they should be rejoicing in the presence of God. If that's you, it's time to be free! You don't need to live that way anymore. The presence of God erases that. There is now no condemnation in Christ Jesus (Romans 8:1), and we don't live at the foot of the cross! We live in its shadow. As a Christian, you already came to the foot of the cross. You got your life right with God. You were washed from the top of your head to the soles of your feet, by the blood of Jesus and now you're living in relationship with Him, in His presence, and that is where you've got to live. What we should be doing is standing at the door of the cross shouting to the masses, "Come, come, come" and bringing them to the foot of the cross, into a relationship with God.

This cycle can also be seen in many marriages. A lot of times, when people have struggles in their marriages, they expect the other one to woo them again, as though they were just starting to date. They act as though they have the option to just hit the road if they don't like the dinner that's set before them or if they don't like a decision the other person made. It's the same with our relationship with God. If every time we didn't agree on something, my wife treated me like I needed to woo her again, it would be a mess. That's not how marriage works. I love my wife and she loves me. We are in a relationship, so even if we don't agree on something, we can talk it out knowing that we're looking out for the best interest of the other. Neither of us has to go outside of the boundaries of our marriage for that. It's exactly like that with our relationship with God! You see people get snatched right out of their marriages in the same cycle that people get in with God, leaving the shadow of the cross to go back out into the world and then come back to the foot again. Don't leave the presence of God to go out and tell Him everything you did wrong. All you have to do is look up and tell Him. He's right there! We don't need to go chasing after Him in dark areas. Even if that's all you've known, that doesn't mean it's all that's available. What's available to you is relationship. Your Father is waiting to hear your voice. It's what He longs for. We are His pride and joy, created to worship Him. If your child disobeyed you, you wouldn't say to them, "You know what. I'm not sure you can stay here anymore." If a five-year-old colors on your wall, you're not going to kick them out of your house. You're going to say, "I forgive you, because I love you." You're going to be frustrated because they did something wrong, but that won't change your love for them. Can you imagine how much more the Father is waiting to do the same thing for us?

- 3 -

BREATHE of GOD

These last days, it's absolutely essential that we live in the power of God. If you feel like your life is stale and powerless, the breath of God will change that and that's what we're going to talk about this chapter. As believers, we all have the potential to walk in dominion and victory, but that doesn't mean that everyone who proclaims the name of God is living in that truth. We do not have to live in a place of fear or concern about what is going on in the world as we quickly race toward the end of time. I believe God is going to call the church out of here before the fullness of the tribulation comes, because if He didn't, then the church would have to be stripped of her dominion authority to allow for the rise of the antichrist and the Bible doesn't teach that. As long as the church is here on the earth, darkness cannot overtake the light!

To understand the power of the breath of God's presence, you need to realize there are different types of people in the Word of God and right now we're going to discuss three people who experienced God's presence in the Word of God.

Let's start all the way back at the beginning. When God created the world, He took the dust of the earth and created Adam. However, that's not where Adam's life came from. God *breathed* into him and that was how Adam was able to take his first breathe. God's very presence was Adam's first inhale. God then put him to sleep, took a rib from him, and created a woman to be his companion.

When they were created, man lived with the breath of God's presence dwelling inside of them. The Bible says that God walked with them in the cool of the day. What did that look like? The Father has no earthly form, so when it says that He walked with them in the cool of the day, it means they had unity. Have you ever wondered how Adam was able to name all of those animals? Well, he had the breath of the presence of God in him, so every time he spoke, not only did he release the word of God, but he released the presence of God. There was creativity and life in everything he did! There was no sin on the earth at this point and there was perfect intimacy between man and God. Unfortunately, though, things went wrong. Most of us will know the story: The serpent came into the garden and caused Adam and Eve to question the very two things I just mentioned— the word and presence of God. He said, "Did God actually say, 'You shall not eat of any tree in the garden?' Eve responded, "We may eat of the fruit of the trees in the garden, but God said, You shall not eat of the fruit of the tree that is in the midst of the garden, neither shall you touch it, lest you die'" (Genesis 3:1-3)? She confirmed what God had said to them. At that point, the deceiver realized that he couldn't defeat her regarding the Word of God, because she was standing firm. So, the serpent changed tactics and went on to say, "You will not surely die. For God knows that when you eat of it your eyes will be opened, and you will be like God, knowing good and evil" (Genesis 3:4-5). This is a very interesting statement because *they were already like God.* However, the serpent brought into question

who they were and deceived them into believing that they were
not like God. Now, I'm not saying they *were* God, but they were
like Him, made in His image, completely unmarred by sin, and
in perfect unity with Him. The very breath of their Creator was
on the inside of them! However, when they believed the serpent
and ate of the forbidden fruit, that intimacy was stripped from
them. When they disobeyed, life in God's presence, which was
all they'd ever known, was taken away. From that moment until
Jesus stepped onto the scene, there was a broken relationship
between God and man. God essentially had to start all over again
by building a foundation through His word; demonstrating who
He is; inviting humanity to know Him; and teaching them how to
be in fellowship with Him.

In the Old Testament, He did this by allowing people to
encounter Him through His name. At the end of Genesis 4, the
word of God says, "At that time people began to call upon the name
of Jehovah" (vs. 26). The process was begun. When Moses had an
encounter with God, he cried out, "Show me your Glory." God
responded, "I will make all my goodness pass before you and will
proclaim before you my name 'Jehovah.' And I will be gracious
to whom I will be gracious and will show mercy on whom I will
show mercy" (Exodus 33:18-19). He declared His name to Moses
and showed him His character. See, God's character and His
name are tied together, just like your character and your name
are tied together. When David went before Goliath he said, "You
come to me with a sword and with a spear and with a javelin,
but I come to you *in the name of Jehovah, the God of the armies of
Israel*, whom you have defied." (1 Samuel 17:45). When the Queen
of Sheba came to Solomon, it doesn't say she came to see all of
his riches, although she was amazed. The Bible says, "When the
queen of Sheba heard of the fame of Solomon *concerning the name*

of Jehovah, she came to test him with hard questions" (1 Kings 10:1).
Solomon was known because he had encountered God through
His name! Jeremiah also encountered God in the power of His
name. He said in Jeremiah 20:9,

"If I say, "I will not mention Him,
or speak any more in His name,"
there is in my heart as it were a burning fire
shut up in my bones,
and I am weary with holding it in,
and I cannot."

Now, they didn't even have what we have today, but the
majority of the people didn't even want to have what they had.
When Moses and the people of Israel came to Mount Sinai, the
Bible says that they were afraid of God's presence and told Moses
to go up for them. They wanted a mediator! God was calling them
unto himself, with a desire to bring them back to the fellowship
they had in the garden of Eden, but they said no! The Bible talks
about those that have a form of godliness, but no substance. We
see this throughout the Scripture! There are those that look and
sound good. They think if they just do what they have to do,
everything will be okay. They keep the law, bring a sacrifice, and
do what they think they have to do to appease God. Throughout
the Scriptures, we see Him continuously telling His people it
doesn't work like that. So, what was it that kept the people we
talked about like Moses, David, and the prophets, serving God?
What was it that captured their hearts?

It was the intimacy of relationship that God has longed for
since the garden. They had the name of the Father being built
into them. They had a powerful foundation, and the presence

of God would come upon them. However, it was very rare in the Old Testament that the Holy Spirit would come and dwell on the inside of them. There are rare occasions in the Bible where the Hebrew would translate to the Spirit of God "putting someone on like clothing," meaning He went inside of them. However, the majority of the time, He would come upon them, and they would release whatever it was God was saying and then His presence would come into agreement with the Word.

In the New Testament, Paul talks about an experience of being "caught up to the third heaven—whether in the body or out of the body" (2 Corinthians 12:2). I really believe this is what the men and women who encountered God in the Old Testament experienced. I believe they had *throne room* experiences. I don't know if they were physically translated somewhere or if it was like when Stephen looked up and saw Jesus at the Father's side. We know from what Moses relayed to the people that He must have seen into Glory. He saw what the tabernacle, with all of its intricate details, looked like. God showed him a picture of the original in Heaven, so he could make a copy of it here on earth.

We also know that the prophets saw into Heaven. The Bible tells us that Jeremiah sat in the counsel of the LORD, and this verbiage is used multiple times in the books of the prophets. The prophets sat and listened with their own ears to what God was saying needed to be said on the earth. Isaiah saw into the throne room of heaven, with the train of the Lord's robe filling the temple! An angel took a coal from the altar of heaven and touched his very lips! They had encounters with God, but they would go in and they would come out. It was not a continuous thing. It wasn't a place that they could dwell continuously. Do you realize that we have the opportunity to dwell in the place they had to leave?

I live on land that has been in my family since the 1800's. My mother lives on the property adjacent to mine where the old farmhouse used to be. The house has since been torn down, but the foundation is still there. I can go and see it, but I can't live there, because it's not a whole house. There's no structure or protection. I can see where the front porch was and imagine what it would have looked like, but it's not a house! God built a foundation from Genesis to Malachi. In the same way that I can't live in the foundation of the old farmhouse, we can't live in that foundation! So many people try living just like this. Often, it's people from older generations that were raised in a particular religious background—maybe Catholic, Baptist, or Methodist. They have a good foundation and a form of Godliness. However, they aren't living in the fullness of truth. Even so, these people have enough of the Bible in them that they will rise up to defend truth without even realizing. They will avoid things that contradict God's word without even knowing why. An example of this is globalism. There are people that don't serve God, but they still have enough of the Bible in them to not want anything to do with the global agenda. It's not a religion of patriotism, which is how many are trying to label it. It's people that have enough of a foundation in Biblical principles to know right from wrong. They may not even know why, but they know they don't want a one world government or one world order. That foundation is a great thing, but so many people live here, and it's not enough.

You have to realize that when Jesus stepped onto the scene, He didn't do away with the foundation. He didn't use a jackhammer on it and throw it out. He built upon it! Do you know that 80-85% of the Bible is the Old Testament? A lot of people degrade the value of the Old Testament, even if they don't realize they're doing it. Many of them end up becoming like King Cyrus of the Bible, who was a Zoroastrian, believing in a "good god" and a "bad god."

They compare the "bad God" of the Old Testament to the "good God" of the New Testament, which is completely ridiculous!

Jesus came as the Second Adam, completely perfect and without sin. When John the Baptist baptized Him, the Holy Spirit descended upon Him like a dove, and the Father spoke from heaven. He then walked out the rest of His mission in absolute unity with the Holy Spirit. He said, "Truly, truly, I say to you, the Son can do nothing of His own accord, but only what He sees the Father doing. For whatever the Father does, that the Son does likewise" (John 5:19).

Now, Jesus called His disciples to come follow Him as He fulfilled His earthly ministry, and these men would have been educated in the law and the Old Testament. They had a Godly foundation, but He gave them more. When He sent them out to minister, He gave them a weapon for their arsenal—*His name*. They returned with joy, saying, "Lord, even the demons are subject to us *in Your name*" (Luke 10:17). He responded, "Nevertheless, do not rejoice in this, that the spirits are subject to you, but rejoice that your names are written in heaven" (Luke 10:20). In other words, Jesus reminded them not to get sidetracked! This is interesting because there are stories recorded of the disciples rejoicing over what they did and arguing over which one of them was the greatest (Mark 9:33-34). They had experienced more than anyone in the Old Testament ever had. They'd experienced more than John the Baptist ever had. However, even after following Jesus for as long as they had and receiving what they did from Him, they were still missing something. Mark 9 tells the story of a demon-possessed boy who was brought to the disciples, but they were unable to cast it out. After Jesus had set Him free, the disciples privately asked Him why they couldn't cast it out. He told them that kind only came out by prayer and fasting. Now, we know they weren't fasting at that time because Jesus said the groomsmen shouldn't fast while the bridegroom was with them (Matthew 9:15)! However, the point of this was that even when the disciples were walking with Jesus, *they needed more!*

They had the foundation of the Old Testament. Jesus had discipled them and given them His name. He was building the house brick by brick, but it wasn't complete yet. Have you ever been in a house without furniture? It feels empty, cold, and lifeless. It echoes. If you've ever been shopping for a house, you know there is a difference between walking into a house staged with furniture and walking into an empty one. A house full of memories, even if they're someone else's memories, feels more alive than a hollow home.

A lot of people live in spiritual houses just like that. They go to church every Sunday. They may go to Bible study on Wednesdays. They've got a great structure, but it's not filled—it's hollow and empty. At the end of the Book of John, after Jesus had been crucified, buried, and resurrected, He said to them, "'Peace be with you. As the Father has sent me, even so I am sending you.' And when He had said this, He breathed on them and said to them, "Receive the Holy Spirit"' (John 20:21-22). At that point, He brought them back to the Garden experience, where the breath of His presence could dwell *in* them.

In Acts 2, we have the story of those same disciples praying in the upper room during the feast of Pentecost and the Holy Spirit fell on them and they were *filled.* The breath of His presence filled the house they were in and filled *them.* That kind of encounter with God will absolutely change your life. When that happens in your life, everything you say will carry power because the breath of God, His very presence, is on the inside of you. When you speak His word, His Spirit comes into immediate agreement. Look at what happened in Acts after the Holy Spirit came! Immediately after the believers were filled, they went out to the streets, and everyone heard God being glorified in their own language. Peter stood up and released the word and presence of God and over 3,000 people were saved.

Too many people today are walking around like empty houses. They have a foundation and a structure, but they aren't filled with the presence of God. They haven't allowed God to breathe His life into them. They may get a little touch from God. They may have an emotional response during worship. They have *something*, but it's never internal. It never breeds intimacy. They never get to know God and allow God to know them in a real personal way. When the Holy Spirit is upon you, on the outside, that is for others. However, when you allow Him to move on the inside of you, a life of dominion starts. That is the place that a life of victory begins. As I said before, the prophets could go in and out of God's presence. He would take them into the throne room and show them things, so they could go out and speak to the people. However, we have something better! We get to live continually seated in heavenly places in Christ Jesus (Ephesians 1:20). We can have a continual throne room experience. The breath of His presence dwells on the inside of us! We never have to leave. We don't leave and gratify the works of the flesh! We don't have to struggle with vices and sin. We don't have to battle fear. We don't have to sit in confusion, not knowing what God wants us to do. We can live with clear direction, understanding, and boldness. There is authority in understanding that the breath of His presence dwells on the inside of us. We don't have to walk in condemnation or guilt. Sadly, many people never reach this place. God does something on the inside of them that lasts for a little while, but then begins to wear off, because it was just a sign of something greater.

Think about it this way: If your car runs out of gas when you're on the side of the interstate and someone comes with one of those little gas cans, that will get your car running! It will get you so far, but that's not enough. It's not actually filling up your tank but is just enough to get you to the place you to go to be filled. This is how a lot of people live! They receive just a touch, just enough gas to keep going, to get them through the situation they're in. However, let's be honest, a lot of people will then forget about God until the next situation. They'll forget about Him until they're on the side of the interstate and they need another touch. We have to take the time, be responsible, and entirely be filled to receive lasting power, lasting victory, and true dominion. Even in that, it has to be continuous. The Bible doesn't say to continuously receive just enough to survive. It says to be continuously filled. Full means being filled to the top and running over! Full doesn't mean a half tank. If you're at a half tank, you're not where you're supposed to be! Full means you have enough plus some for others. There is so much power in knowing who you are, knowing how to get into the word, and pushing forward. When the Holy Spirit begins to move upon you, don't just take a little. When He begins to move, it's a sign of something greater in the room. God wants you to be continually seated in heavenly places with Christ Jesus. There is more!

In the Book of Revelation, John wrote a letter to the church in Ephesus. In it, he said,

"Remember therefore from where you have fallen; repent and do the works you did at first. If not, I will come to you and remove your lampstand from its place, unless you repent" (Revelation 2:5).

Just like Adam and Eve, Jonah, and Moses, the Ephesians had pushed aside the presence of God. In doing that, they demoted themselves from His throne room, but it wasn't hopeless! They were encouraged to repent and do what they did at first, when they first allowed the breath of His presence to fill them. The Bible says that we need to be continuously filled (Ephesians 5:18)! It's not a one-time filling. You leak! You *must* be filled to overflowing, from the top of your head to the soles of your feet, *continuously!* It's the only way you'll walk in dominion. You won't walk in dominion because you think right. You walk in dominion because the Holy Spirit dwells on the inside of You and you obey what He tells you to do. You measure fullness by overflow and God wants to get you into a place of continuous fullness. He doesn't want His presence to just be on you, but His breath to be in you!

Right now, I encourage you to pray this prayer out loud:

"Father right now, I ask You to breathe on me and fill me to overflowing. I don't want just a touch that I can feel on the outside, but something that fills me in the depth of my soul. Empower me and let me know that I am full of Your Holy Spirit. Help me to walk in dominion authority and to know that I am seated in heavenly places in the throne room of God. Remind me now that nothing can demote me from Your presence except my own decisions. No outside force can separate me from You. Help me to dwell in Your presence continually from this day forward. Let me be continually full of Your power, love, and stability as Your word says. I ask you to eradicate all fear, shame, guilt, and condemnation. Let Your presence fill every area of my heart that has been afraid to receive it. Thank you, Father, that it's Your good pleasure to give me the kingdom and every good gift that You have. Give me the confidence to do what You have put me on the earth to do. Amen!

- 4 -

COVENANT of GOD'S PRESENCE

Many people don't realize that there are signs of God's covenants, and this is important to understand when you talk about His presence. Right now, we're going to deal with just three of the signs that we can see in Scripture.

The first sign of the covenant in the Bible is the rainbow, which was a sign from God to man that He would never flood the Earth in judgement again. It doesn't mean it won't rain. It doesn't mean there won't be flooding, but there is a promise that we have from God that He will never entirely destroy the Earth by flood again. That promise is for us every time we see a rainbow in the sky. Another sign of the covenant that God has given mankind is the Sabbath—the day of rest. God worked for six days, creating the heavens and the Earth and on the seventh day, He rested. The Sabbath, according to the Word of God, is actually a sign of our sanctification. The Sabbath itself does not sanctify us spiritually but is a sign that we are sanctified unto Him. From science, we understand that rest causes toxins to be released and allows time for your body to heal. You will be revitalized by the Sabbath, both physically and spiritually. The third sign of the covenant that I want to talk about is circumcision. Circumcision began with Abraham, and it was a sign so that every circumcised male would be reminded several times a day that he is in covenant with God. Again, these things are not the covenant, but serve as signs pointing to the promise of something greater.

Unfortunately, many people misunderstand the purpose of the signs. Even in the Old Testament, people didn't understand why the Israelites circumcised their males. People misunderstood the Sabbath. It doesn't make sense, in the natural, to only work six days a week when you can make more money working seven. People would get frustrated, because they would place their trust in the sign they didn't understand, instead of in God. They would argue and debate and completely miss God's purpose. As soon as the Sabbath was over, they would rush to open their shops to make money. Jeremiah addressed this when he talked about the people being "circumcised in body, but uncircumcised in heart!" He said in Jeremiah 4:4,

> "Circumcise yourselves to the LORD.
> remove the foreskin of your hearts,
> O men of Judah and inhabitants of Jerusalem.
> lest my wrath go forth like fire,
> and burn with none to quench it,
> because of the evil of your deeds!"

Paul dealt with this in the New Testament, especially regarding circumcision, because the people still didn't understand that circumcision was not the covenant, but simply a sign. Paul told them that if they didn't have circumcision of the heart, then their circumcision of the flesh meant nothing. This was not a new idea in the New Testament!

Now, where I live there's a particular sign that means a lot to me and it says, "Skyline Chili." If you're not from the Cincinnati area, that means nothing to you, but when I see that sign, I feel a gravitational pull toward the restaurant. It's one of my favorite foods and if I have to drive past the sign, it's painful. I know what is in that restaurant and I can almost taste the food in mouth when I get close. However, even when I see the sign and I know exactly what is waiting for me inside, that doesn't satisfy me. Once you have tasted what a sign points to, the sign itself will never be enough. We have been in church long enough to see people chase signs. I've seen people chase signs all over the world, in all honesty. I attend an incredible church that allows the working of the Holy Spirit without measure. However, I've seen people leave that atmosphere to go to chase signs that they hear about, whatever they may be. Throughout the years, it's been feathers, gold dust, and all kinds of other things. Now, I don't believe there's anything wrong with those things! I believe that God manifests Himself in different, miraculous ways. However, it's sad that people leave a place where the Holy Spirit is welcome to move, just for the sake of chasing a sign. The purpose of the signs of the covenant that God has given are to make us hungry for more! All of the things that God does to point to a greater reality are not meant to satisfy you. If you put more emphasis on the signs that God gives than on His presence, you will end up in trouble. Your hope cannot be placed more on a sign than on the God who gives it!

So, what exactly are all of those signs of the covenant pointing to? They point to *Him* and the covenant of His presence that He has given to us, as believers. The Bible says in Hebrews 13:5-6,

"I will never leave you nor forsake you."

So, we can confidently say,
"The Lord is my helper.
I will not fear.
what can man do to me?"

Jesus said that He had to go away so that the comforter, the Holy Spirit, could come (John 16:7). Joel 2:28-29 records the powerful prophecy,

"And it shall come to pass afterward,
that I will pour out my Spirit on all flesh.
your sons and your daughters shall prophesy,
your old men shall dream dreams,
and your young men shall see visions.
Even on the male and female servants
in those days I will pour out my Spirit."

It spoke of a time that the Spirit of God would be poured out on *all flesh!* This was fulfilled in Acts 2! Peter quoted Joel in Acts 2:15 saying, "For these people are not drunk, as you suppose, since it is only the third hour of the day. But this is what was uttered through the prophet Joel." We have this promise, this covenant, that God has done what He said He would and given us His presence! We have continual access to the presence of God.

I was just talking to someone recently who had been going to a church for five years. I'm not going to mention the church, but they said they could count just a handful of times in that time that the presence of God had invaded the place, and something happened. My question to them was, "why are you still there?" I'm not trying to be harsh, but you have the promise of God that the Holy Spirit can live on the inside of you. You have the covenant promise that the very breathe of the presence of God can dwell in you. Church is supposed to be a place to encounter that presence! If I was in a church where nothing happened, where the Spirit of God was not allowed to move, I would honestly pack up my family, quit my job, and move across the country, if necessary, to find a place that was experiencing a move of God's presence. A church without the presence of God will have to come up with other ways to keep you there. They may have good programs, good music, and good coffee. There's nothing wrong with those things, but there is no substitute for His presence! I've heard it all! I've talked to people who made excuses for leaving a church where God was moving because there was a good program for their kids. Then a few years later, their kids were completely spiritually dead because it was just games. They had fun, but there was no substance. There was no presence of God, no meat of the Word, and no lasting fruit. Without the presence of God, a place may look great, but it's just an illusion!

Something I really enjoy doing is watching "magicians." I really enjoy watching them perform their illusions. Interestingly enough, there were illusionists all the way back in Jesus' day. Historians tell us of temple doors opening and closing on their own, but this wasn't supernatural. During the 100 years prior to the temple being destroyed, the priests were not legitimate, and God was not moving. To ensure the people didn't lose interest, the priests came up with illusions to make the people think that God was moving. You see this throughout history with false gods as well. They would have tricks, such as a booming voice coming out of a statue that would make people believe there was power when there was none.

I just watched one of these illusionists the other day. In a public place, a man spilled coffee on a girl (both of whom were part of the prank). The girl acted upset, threw him backwards and then up a wall using what looked like the force from Star Wars. She then turned around to the people who were not in on the prank acting angry. She threw her arms out and tables went flying, books fell off the bookcase and picture frames flew off the wall. Now all of this was a set up but none of the people there knew that it was an illusion, so they were terrified! How easily the people believed it was real! It was just a creative trick, but no one could see that, because of the excellence of the illusion.

Is it any wonder then the Bible says that in the last day, there will be signs and wonders that will deceive "even the elect" (Matthew 24:24)? Signs and wonders are real! They point to an all-powerful, wonderworking God. However, you can never follow signs! If a man or a woman preaches and signs or wonders break out, that tells you very little about them. It does tell you a whole lot about God, though! God will always back up His word. However, when people don't have that power, they have to do something counterfeit to keep people interested and get them to come back.

Far too often, people put the cart in front of the horse. The horse pulling the cart is supposed to be the word of God. You are in the seat of the cart, pushing the Word of God out in front of you and hiding behind it. Directly behind you, in the cart, are all of the things that God says we can have. Signs, wonders, blessings, and prosperity are all in the cart, following you! These aren't the main thing, but they are a thing that has been promised!

When you have a good sports team, there will be times that they do an unusual play, in the last minute of the game and it's down to the wire. In those last moments, they may be able to pull an incredible play out that's out of the ordinary, to push through to win. Any team that's going to be successful, though, has to have a solid strategy. That last minute, incredible play didn't come out of nowhere. They must have worked hard and prepared before game day. There had to have been a plan for them to get to that place to be able to pull a power play out as a team. This is similar to the way we should be with the word of God. We can't rely on signs and wonders to carry us, although we should be thankful for them and expect to see them. They should not be our strategy. We should expect to see these things because God has given us that promise. However, our playbook, the way that we study and the way that we prepare has to come straight from the word of God. Even though it looks like it, those extraordinary plays don't come from the heat of the moment, but from lots of preparation and practice, and it will be the same way in your life!

There are rewards for those who diligently seek God. The Bible says that "signs and wonders follow those who believe" (Mark 16:17)! It doesn't say those who believe chase signs and wonders all over the earth. Signs and wonders are extremely important, but they should never be your focus, or you will get deceived and led off into things that don't matter. You have to realize that the main thing always should be the presence of God dwelling on the inside of you and pouring forth out of you to touch a desperate world! Push the word of God out in front of you and hide behind it. No matter what is going on in the world, in society or in culture, the word of God never changes!

Whether the sign is the Sabbath, circumcision, or the rainbow, the purpose of it is to point to a greater reality. Even Jesus Himself came to point mankind back to the Father and the reality of the Kingdom of Heaven. It was His whole goal. Jesus came and died on the cross so that we could have a relationship with His Daddy. He came so that His Father could be our Father. That's now our purpose! Our lives should point to that greater reality, too! We should always be pointing to the author and finisher of our faith.

He's the one who can save us from every ounce of destruction. Our lives should also point to the Father. If you create a Christian culture, solely focused on Jesus and neglecting the Father, all you will do is create a bunch of spiritual orphans. We have to have the fullness of the gospel—the entire counsel of the Word of God.

Again, don't misunderstand me here. Signs and wonders are important! They must accompany the preaching of the word of God, and they should follow the believer. If signs are not following you, something is wrong, but keep the main thing the main thing! A few years ago, I went with an evangelist to a church. One of the associate pastors of the church wanted to hear some stories and they were great stories! He talked about all the things he wanted to see. I sat there just listening like a fly on a wall, as the evangelist tried to tell him what I'm sharing right now. Then the Evangelist asked me what I thought about it. I was taken off guard for a second, but I looked at him and was able to respond without hesitation. I said, "I don't care if I ever see gold dust, feathers, or any of those other signs. I don't care if I ever see someone get healed. I don't care if I ever see someone get saved." Hear me out! I said, "All I care about is falling more in love with my God, every single day." See, when I do that, then all of the other things have to follow me. The signs, the healings, and the salvations! We have to keep the main thing the main thing. I have to be in relationship with the Holy Spirit. I have to be in relationship with the One who convicts and guides me. For a lot of people, God is just a concept and an idea, but He's more real than our next breathe. When the Holy Spirit comes in, He will convict and challenge us. *That's how change happens.* We have to allow the presence of God to come into our lives! God never convicts us to condemn us. He doesn't want to embarrass us. He doesn't desire to shame us. He convicts us so that we can be healed. However, if you have a mental concept of God, but you push away His conviction when it comes, then you'll never change. You'll push away the presence of God and all that will remain is your idea of God in your own limited understanding. This will just be a religious fuel for you to argue with those who disagree with you. That's what happens when you reject God's presence! This is why it's so important that we allow God to deal with us. He's given us the covenant of His presence. He will never leave us. He will never forsake us.

If you look around, you will see that God is moving. There was a man holding meetings in the state of California in the midst of lockdowns and people were being saved, healed, and delivered in multitudes. This man's first crusade was when he was 12 years old and he had 10,000 people in attendance. In another crusade, while he was speaking, a woman brought a child to him. She threw the child at his feet, and said, "if what you're saying is true, then heal my child. Otherwise, stop now, because no one here will believe you." He picked the child up in his arms and the child was healed, instantly. God loves people! He wants people to encounter Him. This is the day of the greatest harvest that the church has ever seen. We can't sit on the sidelines and do nothing and expect the government to back us up. It's not going to happen! Listen, I plan to be on the first train out of here. I'm not going to be waiting around to see this world go crazy. There is a restraining that is happening on the earth right now and it's because of the Church of Jesus Christ. We are currently restraining the expansion of the kingdom of darkness. I refuse to believe that anything is getting worse! I believe the greatest days of the church are ahead of us, not behind us. There is a great harvest coming. Revival is now! We have to be the church. We have to be the change that we want to see. We have to do it through the power of the Holy Spirit! We have to do it through the presence of God coming and dwelling in us and being released to the hungry world around us. When we speak the word of God, the Holy Spirit will come into agreement, and we'll see the change we declare.

On the day of Pentecost, the Holy Spirit fell and everyone in that room spoke in other tongues. As you read through the book of Acts, this sign accompanied the Holy Spirit when He fell on people. When God comes to dwell on the inside of you, your vocabulary will change. The Holy Spirit will change how you think and speak and one aspect of this is speaking in tongues, also referred to as your prayer language, or glossolalia! We have to remember that while tongues is a sign of the Holy Spirit, it is not the Holy Spirit. You could speak in tongues but end up as lost as a goose in a snowstorm. Speaking in tongues is a good thing! I do it every day. It focuses and empowers me. It's a gift to the believer and God wants every single person filled with the Holy Spirit with the evidence of speaking in tongues! However, it is not the covenant. Speaking in tongues is not the presence of God. Speaking in tongues is a *sign* of His presence and there are many signs of the Holy Spirit!

God's word does not return to Him void. I have seen people who are not living right preach the Word of God and see things happen. God will always stand behind His Word, and that's why you cannot follow signs. You have to know the character of a person. You can't go based on what someone says, but how they live their life. You may think that what they're doing really works and it may work for a season! However, that season will come to an end. Charisma, signs, and wonders may work for a time, but they will not sustain you. God will share His glory with no one, so if someone's life does not come into agreement with His word, what they've built will come crashing down. Your character must line up with the word of God!

Always remember that signs and wonders point to a greater reality and while they aren't the main thing, it's not wrong to ask for them. Last year, I got to the place that I began to ask God to move in greater ways in some situations. It was a desire borne out of my relationship with Him. The Holy Spirit comes on the inside of you for you, but He comes upon you for others and it's not wrong to ask God to do things! As I prayed, I began to see God move in a greater way! We watched legs grow out; backs be healed; and people get touched by the Holy Spirit. We don't chase signs and wonders. However, you can't just sit around doing nothing and say you're waiting on God. You've got to take the word of God and let it be activated by faith and move forward with the presence of God in you. If you don't have signs following you, then you're doing something wrong. One of the greatest miracles that God can do is to take a man out of darkness, purify him, and then put him back into the situation he came from and keep him clean. If you want to talk to God about power, He's going to talk to you about purity! You can't live a compromised life and expect the presence of God to dwell in you and signs and wonders to follow you. If you decide to compromise, even a little bit, the Holy Spirit and the presence of God will take a step back and will have nothing to do with it. You will eventually hit rock bottom. God hates compromise. It is the little leaven that leavens the whole loaf of bread and it's the little foxes that spoil the vine. It doesn't take a lot. You can't think to yourself that you can get away with just a little bit of sin or a little bit of compromise. Jesus told people on multiple occasions "go and sin no more!" If He said this, it means we have the ability to live in victory over sin! We can live a holy life, totally and completely free. The ideology that you can live however you want, and that grace will cover it, is nowhere in the word of God! Many people don't want to count the cost. They don't want to pay the price. They will come up with excuses for why they live powerless lives. They'll say the Holy Spirit was just for the apostles. They'll say miracles were just for the birth of the church and not for now. They got to me too late! My wife was born with a birth defect and was told she wouldn't be able to walk by the time she was 25. I can tell you that she is more than 25 years old and has been completely healed of that defect for years! We've seen miracle after miracle, in her life and in the lives of people around us. It starts with *you*. It starts with intimacy with God and a life bathed in His presence. Signs, wonders, and miracles are not the main thing, but they inevitably follow the believer who walks in covenant with God!

- 5 -

GOD'S WORD
and PRESENCE

One thing you need to understand is that creation is at the heart of God's nature. In the book of Genesis, one of the first things we see God do is to create by the power of His word. Words, in general, can be used for a lot of different things. Most people use them primarily for communication, but our words can do far more than that! Your word can also create, just like God's can. They can cultivate an atmosphere around you that is just like the world—full of shame, guilt, and negativity—or an atmosphere of the presence of God. That's what we're going to be dealing with in the coming pages.

Numbers 20 records the story of the people of Israel at the waters of Meribah. The Bible says that at this place, the people quarreled with Moses and Aaron. The people's words created an atmosphere of negativity. At this point, the Bible says that Moses left that negative atmosphere of the people and entered into the presence of God. God brought His presence down by His word. You have to understand that the word of God and the presence of God are one. When the presence of God shows up, it is His word! God spoke to Moses and commanded him to speak to the rock and tell it to bring forth water. The problem was that Moses had no reference point for this. Moses had argued with God many times. When the Lord told him to go bring the people up out of Egypt at the burning bush, he argued that he was only a man! He was constantly aware of his own inability, not understanding that God was trying to empower him with His presence upon him.

What kind of words shape the atmosphere that you live in? If you let the news, or anything based in fear, dictate how you think or feel, you will live in a constant atmosphere of negativity. We know a man who was a meteorologist here in the Cincinnati area. His contract came up for renewal and there was some contention. One aspect of his contract was that when he reported the weather, he had to do it in a way that would instill concern in the viewers. Now, this man is a believer and he told them he would not report it that way, so they didn't renew his contract. If they do that with the weather, how much more do you think they try to infuse fear into other aspects of the news? You have to realize that you have a choice in everything that you say and do. My wife told me a story recently about an issue she was dealing with that felt so overwhelming in her mind! She knew it wasn't as big of a deal as it felt, but she was struggling to push past it. That day we worshipped as a family and as soon as we started, God's peace came upon her immediately. Many times, when people are dealing with trials, they use the phrase "que sera sera," which translates to "whatever will be will be." That phrase means that something is out of your control, and you aren't going to worry about it, even if you are still worrying about it! It's a mentality of letting the issue go. On the other hand, when believers are facing trials, they will often say "Come what may," which has a completely different meaning! That's saying, "I will have peace, no matter what." Que sera sera comes from the negative mentality of accepting that anything can happen to you, while *come what may* is from a mentality of abiding in the presence of God. It's realizing that whatever you face, you'll be empowered to move forward with the peace of God. It matters *how* you go forward. Will you go from a place of negativity or positivity? Here in this story, the people of Israel created an atmosphere of negativity by their complaining, but that won't be your story!

It doesn't matter how insignificant a person seems, when the word and the presence of God come into agreement in their lives and they release it, there will be an immediate response. That is how you enact the will of God on the Earth. We see the same principle in the New Testament after Jesus was resurrected. He came back to the disciples, breathed on them, and said, "Receive the Holy Spirit" (John 20:22).

Remember that when they received the Holy Spirit on the day of Pentecost, it was not something that just came upon them. They received the Holy Spirit down on the inside of them and God made a way for all believers to live in that reality! Every believer can have the infilling of the Holy Spirit! After this happened, when they released the Word of God, the presence of God poured out and there was an immediate response. On the day of Pentecost, Peter stood up after being filled with the Holy Spirit and over 3,000 people were cut to the heart by the word and converted. This is what happens when the Word of God and His Spirit agree in a person's life! Every word that you release carries power.

It's so important that you do not speak in contradiction to the word of God. You cannot recite your limitation or defeat. You cannot just constantly rehearse your problems, challenges, and difficulties. What if you began to release the word of God and the presence of God over your situation instead of just talking about the issues around you? Try it and see what begins to happen! You have to understand that not everything is instantaneous. Recently, my wife and I have seen many things come to pass that grew from seeds planted in our hearts years ago. You can't try something for a moment and then say it didn't work! You have to be faithful. The word of God always works.

In Isaiah 6, we read a very interesting story in which Isaiah gets a glimpse into heaven. He's looking into the throne room and sees God lifted up and the train of His robe filling the temple. Isaiah said "'Woe is me! For I am lost; for I am a man of unclean lips, and I dwell in the midst of a people of unclean lips; for my eyes have seen the King, the LORD of hosts" (Isaiah 6:5)! In this verse, we see Isaiah realize his humanity. He became acutely aware of his own inadequacies. He had an understanding when he saw God that he was missing something. He said his lips were unclean and he was in a midst of people with unclean lips. He was not humiliated or belittling himself from a place of condemnation or destruction, but he had a pure humility! He simply became aware of the holiness of God. To be humble is not thinking less of yourself but thinking of yourself less. We see people in Scripture that *did* belittle themselves, like Moses, but that's not what God wants for us. He wants us to be able to say from a humble and pure place "He must increase, and I must die." We need to get to the point that we know that there is no life in the flesh and every selfish desire has to die. In the next verses, Isaiah went on to say,

'Then one of the seraphim flew to me, having in his hand a burning coal that he had taken with tongs from the altar. And he touched my mouth and said: "Behold, this has touched your lips; your guilt is taken away, and your sin atoned for."' (Isaiah 6:6-7)

The Seraphim touched Isaiah's lips with a coal taken from

the altar. We know that what Moses built was after the pattern of what was already in place in heaven. It's very likely that Moses saw a picture of the reality in heaven and made a replica on the Earth. I believe the Seraphim took a coal from an altar meant for sacrifice and when there is a sacrifice, there is blood. You have to understand that the Bible says that Jesus was slain before the foundations of the Earth. I believe the Seraphim took a coal with the blood of the sacrifice of the Son of God that was already in the heart of the Father and touched it to Isaiah's lips. There was blood of atonement on the burning coal! In this way, God was saying, "Your sin is atoned for. Your lips are clean. The words that come out of your mouth will no longer create an unclean presence. You are clean and you will release the presence of God." The truth of atonement will always bring comfort!

The Scripture goes on to say in Isaiah 6:8, 'And I heard the voice of the Lord saying, "Whom shall I send, and who will go for us?" Then I said, "Here I am! Send me."'

There is a calling on everyone's life. You have to understand that God doesn't need a vast army of people to get things done. It only takes one person in a family, a city, a state, or a nation to say, "enough is enough." If you will begin to stand your ground, declaring the Word of the Lord and releasing His presence, you will see change! Don't allow the enemy another foot of ground.

We are not on our way to a great destruction. In these last days, we are on our way to a glorious, triumphant finish. That is what the Church will see, as we step into what God has called us to do. However, we do have the responsibility to step into the mandate God has placed on each of our lives and unfortunately, this is where most people fail. Listen, You can't speak doubt and faith at the same time. You can't say, "well, I believe that, *but...*" Many people will begin speaking faith and get discouraged when the first trial comes.

I remember listening to a man not too terribly long ago. He was telling a story about how God began to do many miraculous things. His ministry was exploding. As that began, his wife was spiritually attacked in her body. Her health began to suffer. He pulled back thinking that if he stopped pushing forward in ministry, the attack would stop and his wife would recover, but it never works that way. The man told me how this went on for a very long time. I wondered what would have happened if he would have continued pressing on. What would have happened if, when the attack from Hell came to try and stop him, he pushed forward with everything he had? When the enemy comes to try to buffer you, what are you going to do? What would happen if instead of easing off when buffering comes, you push forward with everything you have?

Let me give you an example. My wife rides an exercise bike and loves it. This is incredible because she's had so much physical breakthrough and healing. Some of that healing has been miraculous and some has been through God's direction in different areas. My wife was telling me recently about how hard it was to get back on her bike after our vacation. We'd had a great trip and she'd done great physically, but that first day back was *hard*. Exercise requires you to push through if you're going to see a reward, and it's the same way with spiritual things. Sometimes you ride and it's easy because you're in a vein and you feel strong. You're being blessed and things are falling in your favor. We all love those times! However, when things are a little bit harder, when it feels like there's a lot of steep hills and rough terrain, *that's* when the ride takes more effort. There are times when you may feel exhausted or afraid and want to quit. *Those* are the moments that you have to look at the blessing that's come! We have to draw on our history with God and remember who He is and what He's done. Remember where He's brought you from and remind yourself that He will do it again. God's desire is for you to get stronger and stronger. Just like with exercise, sometimes it's difficult, but you can't let those challenges hold you back. You can't stop when things get hard and just get off the bike! Just like we tell our kids, if you take a hit, stand up, shake it off and move forward. You have to understand that if you give the devil an inch, he'll take a mile. *Don't ever let the enemy keep you from moving forward.* It's normal to be challenged, but it's unscriptural to be defeated. Keep pressing on!

One of the most powerful ways to see breakthrough when things are difficult is by releasing your faith in the words that you speak. Your words and the words of the people are around you create a presence. Adam and Eve are a good example of this. They had oneness with God, living so intimately that God walked with them daily. One act of disobedience destroyed that connection. God came into the Garden of Eden where Adam and Eve were attempting to hide from their creator. He said, "Where are you?" to which they responded that they'd hidden themselves because they were naked. He asked them, "Who told you that you were naked?" In other words, He wanted to know what they'd heard that created an atmosphere of shame and made them aware of their own nakedness. That shame broke the intimacy they'd known day in and day out. So many people let one thing sever the connection they had with God. They let one mistake, one trial, tear them from the path they were walking on and keep them from all the things God spoke over them, but it doesn't have to be that way.

The question is, *where are you?* What are you doing with the things God's spoken? Are you living with the intimacy that

God desires or have you allowed yourself to live in the presence of the negativity around you? Are you walking around like you have a rain cloud over your head, in an atmosphere of shame and guilt and fear? Are you allowing your own words to create a negative atmosphere? The moment a born-again believer walks into a room, that place should light up! As Christians, we are not meant to be the thermometers of a room, but the thermostat! We're not supposed to go into a place and decide if it makes us comfortable or not. We are supposed to go into a room and set the temperature by God's presence. We can go into the room and change the atmosphere simply by being there. The grace of God is a sparkling free gift. When you walk in with that grace, full of the Holy Spirit, everyone should feel something different! The lost should become convicted, and drawn to God, without even knowing why. Have you ever had people speak or act differently, just because you're in the room? They may choose not to cuss around you or talk about the things they normally talk about when you haven't said a word. That's because the presence of God changes the atmosphere!

Adam allowed the serpent to speak a lie and create an atmosphere that was not of God and the most tragic part of the story is that Adam had dominion over that serpent the whole time. He could have taken that serpent by the neck and thrown him out of the garden at any moment. Instead, he entertained nonsense. Don't allow lies, negativity, and nonsense into your domain!

Moses argued with God that he couldn't speak well. He had a mindset that he couldn't do it. God responded that He would teach him how to speak, but Moses couldn't receive that truth. When God told him to speak to the rock, is it possible he still had that insecurity? In a moment of anger, instead of obeying God and speaking to the rock, he reverted back to what he'd done before.

He reverted back to what he was comfortable with and struck the rock! For that, he was never allowed to enter the promised land. We have to obey what God is speaking to us to do in every circumstance because He will never ask us to do something without giving us what we need to accomplish it.

Isaiah said that he was unclean, because he was among a people who were unclean, but it doesn't have to be that way. We can be in the world, but not of it! We can be among unclean people but kept clean by the Holy Spirit. God wants us to understand that we can take His word and so consume it that it becomes a part of who we are. We have to pray in the Holy Spirit and allow God to fill us. It's not a one-time filling but a continuous infilling of His presence, until you constantly overflow. When I speak faith, I'm not just saying words out of my mouth. I'm releasing the very Word and presence of God to see breakthrough in every circumstance!

Take care with the words that you speak. Declare the word of God! It's not about being goofy or disconnected from reality. It's speaking the truth of what God has said in faith, believing that it will come to pass. It's believing that you can always be victorious. It's believing that you can be the lender and not the borrower (Deuteronomy 15:6). It's believing you can be the head and not the tail (Deuteronomy28:13). Regardless of the situation you're in, God will bring you out of it and into the exact place you need to be.

I heard a pastor share a story that he went into a store and was paying for something. A woman came up behind him just to get in line and she stood behind them and the power of God hit her, and she fell back. He turned around and saw what had happened and asked God, "What is that?" God responded, "You leaked." That's what it means to go into a place and change the equation! I'm not saying that's the kind of thing that happens very often, but that is the kind of experience you can have if you live in the constant overflow of God's presence. When you're full of His Spirit, something should happen every time you step into a room! You should carry a Holy Ghost boldness to say what God says over every situation and change the atmosphere every place you go! Jesus said, "I only say what I hear the Father saying and do what I see the Father doing" (John 5:19-20). When we begin to do that, it changes the equation! When we begin to do exactly that, with pure boldness, knowing that God is for us, all of heaven will back us up!

- 6 -

the LASTING EVIDENCE
of the HOLY SPIRIT

Throughout this book, we have talked several times about how God doesn't want to just come on you, but He wants to come and dwell on the inside of you. This is what it means to live an empowered life. The Holy Spirit is the only way that we live an empowered life. Now, the initial evidence of the infilling of the Spirit is speaking in tongues, but that is not the lasting effect of the Holy Spirit, which is what we're going to discuss now.

When God told Moses to speak to the rock, which we talked about previously, He wanted him to release a sound. That word would have come into agreement with the presence of God and the Holy Spirit to produce a result. The same is true today! When the word of God and the Holy Spirit agree in your life, there will be powerful results.

When a person is initially immersed in the Holy Spirit, we call it being *baptized in the Holy Spirit*. When you are baptized in water you are fully submerged. In the same way, when you are baptized in the Holy Spirit, He comes and fully immerses you in God's presence and into the newness of the Christian life! Now, you could still choose to set it aside and walk away, but if you choose to accept it and walk in the Holy Spirit, your life will be changed!

As we said before, the initial evidence of the baptism of the Holy Spirit is what is called speaking in tongues. There will be people that disagree with this truth, but we see it several times in the book of Acts. In Acts 2 when the Holy Spirit filled the upper room at Pentecost, divided tongues of fire rested on the head of the disciples, and they began to speak in tongues. The Bible says that the crowds that heard it marveled, because they were hearing the Word of God in their own languages. People had come from many different places, but as the disciples spoke, they all heard it in their native tongues. We see it in also in Acts 10 when Peter visited the house of Cornelius, a gentile. They believed the gospel and were filled with the Holy Spirit and began to speak in tongues, just like the believers did on the day of Pentecost! However, this is only the *initial* sign. Too many people never go deeper into God than this point right here, but you could be filled with the Holy Spirit and not walk in the fullness of what God has for you. I want to share with you a few things from the Word of God and my experience regarding the *lasting* evidence of the baptism of the Holy Spirit.

First of all, I know that some people would disagree with me on this point, but I'm telling you from the Word of God and experience that the baptism of the Holy Spirit is available to every believer. I understand that the Holy Spirit has been poured out on all flesh. Everyone on Earth has a measure of God's Spirit, as we are all made in His image, but that is not what I'm talking about here. I'm talking about the baptism of the Holy Spirit with the evidence of speaking in tongues.

Now, Paul said to the Corinthian church that he spoke in tongues more than all of them (1 Corinthians 14:18). He never downplayed the significance of this initial gift. Smith

Wigglesworth gave some great wisdom on this! He said if you pray in the Holy Spirit for 15 minutes every morning until you feel the anointing—the presence of God— then you will never backslide! I know that to be true! When the presence of God comes, there is a release of His power and a destruction of the yoke of bondage. He builds you up and gives you direction for your life! He gives clarity of mind and peace of heart! There have been scientific tests done in which they hooked people up to monitors so they could watch their brain activity while they were speaking in tongues. These tests confirmed that their brain function was different when they spoke in tongues than when they were just talking or even praying.

When you begin to pray in the Spirit, God will clear your mind and renew it. By His word, He will give you direction and clarity about how to move forward. He will destroy fear, anxiety, and depression. Every form of emotional and mental instability is destroyed by the releasing of the power and presence of God. Praying in tongues builds your spirit up to receive those things that God has for you.

A man with an experience is never at the mercy of a man with an argument. I have had experiences with God I know when His presence comes into a room. When you pray in the Holy Spirit every day, it gives you a sensitivity toward God. The peace and power of God will dwell in your life. When you pray in tongues, your spirit connects with God's Spirit, and He will refresh and recharge you. You need that *daily*! It's a gift we need to use in every level of our walk with God!

While the gift of tongues is a powerful gift, there is more! You can tell by looking at a person's life whether they've continued on in God or if they decided they'd arrived and set up camp when they received the baptism of the Holy Spirit. You can tell by the mentality that a person has whether or not they have a weak baptism. If you have a mentality that you constantly need prayer, you are not walking in the fullness of His Spirit. If you're always struggling to move forward, you have a weak baptism, because that's not the way God wants us to live. Another indicator of a weak baptism is the people you hang around. If you constantly surround yourself with people who live like the world or Christians who don't want anything to do with the moving of God's Spirit, you will limit yourself. Show me your friends and I'll show you your future.

Jesus didn't die on the cross and rip the veil in two so you could stay defeated. He died on the cross and rose from the grave, tearing the veil, so that we could walk in the power of the Holy Spirit! When you come to an understanding of what the word of God says and the Holy Spirit moves on that understanding, it produces faith. When faith is activated by the works that you do, it brings a new level of dominion and victory in your life. Faith without works is dead! If you are constantly struggling, taking one step forward and two steps back, there's a problem. Listen, I understand trials come, but you have to understand that while it's normal to be challenged, it is unscriptural to be defeated.

Ephesians 5:18 says, "And do not get drunk with wine, for that is debauchery, but be filled with the Spirit." The word used for "filled" in that Scripture in its original language does not indicate a one-time infilling. A better translation would actually say "be continuously filled" with the Holy Spirit. We are earthen vessels and earthen vessels leak. You can't just be filled once a week or once a month. You must be filled with the Holy Spirit constantly! If you tried to drive a car day after day and never put fuel in it, would you be surprised when it ran out and you couldn't take it anywhere? Your life is no different. If you do run out of gas though, all you have to do is fill it up! You don't need a mechanic or a new car. You just need gas and to get going. In the same way, you need a fresh filling of the Holy Spirit every day! To continue with the car analogy, you could also end up on the side of the road because you don't do your regular maintenance. If you don't ever change the oil on your car, it will run and run until one day the engine just locks up. That's what will happen if you reject the presence and power of God. Your walk with God will come to a halting stop and you'll need some serious repair to get moving again! If you don't spend time doing the regular maintenance—reading the Word, praying, and being with God—you will break down. The Word of God, who is Jesus, is called our daily bread. We need His presence *daily*. You don't eat just one time and never go back to it. We also don't eat just once a month or even once a week or a day. We eat several times a day or we weaken! Our bodies are made to need food and our spirits are made to live by His presence.

Any time you start something healthy, our gains can seem slow in comparison to other things. When you begin a new workout regimen, for example, the first workout is *hard*. It would be great if we saw results immediately, but it takes time and consistency to see fruit. Our spiritual health is no different, but every time you do something healthy, every time you pray in tongues or spend time in the word, you're getting stronger! The moment you stop putting in the work, you will begin to get weaker. You may not immediately notice the changes, but after some time you'll realize you can't do what you used to be able to do. You'll realize your faith isn't what it used to be, your strength and your desire for the things that are good for you will wither away. So, if you find yourself in a place where your passion is dimmed, *do what you know is good for you*. If you don't feel like reading the word, *do it anyway*. If you don't feel like praying in tongues, *do it anyway*. If you don't *feel* like it, that's all the more reason to do it!

I saw a post on social media recently that asked how people deal with stress. Now, I'm not being facetious when I say that I thought to myself "What stress?" I refuse to live in stress. I'm not saying stress won't try to come in, but I have learned how to quickly deal with it. I don't let it hang around while I come up with coping methods. I go to God, and I say, "God, whatever you want me to do or say in this situation, I'll do it, but I know I've got seed in the ground and I'm doing what you've told me to do, so I trust you to take care of this." I may pray in the Spirit or spend time in the Word. I get myself in God's presence until I feel the pressure lift. If you trust God with something, there is no sense in continuing to fret about it. You don't want to allow things to build up in your life. The longer you allow a burden to remain, the weaker you'll become. Don't push off your prayer time or your time with God! If you continue to push it off, you'll go from getting into the Word every day, to once a week, to once a month, until you won't remember the last time you spent time in His word! Don't allow it to happen. Very rarely do these things happen like a blowout; they're usually slow leaks! You have to be continually being filled!

Now, I want to share with you three things that happen when you allow God to continually fill you. These can all be found in 2 Timothy 1:6-7 which says,

"For this reason, I remind you to fan into flame the gift of God, which is in you through the laying on of my hands, for God gave us a spirit not of fear but of power and love and self-control."

The first thing I want you to realize here is that fear is not something that God hands to anyone. It's never from Him. I understand people face challenges, but if you're struggling with the same thing for years on end, something is wrong. You've got to figure out what the disconnect it! The Bible says that perfect love casts out fear (1 John 4:18) and in the Scripture above we see that not only has God not given us fear, but He has given us *power, love, and a sound mind.* One of the things God gives us when He fills us with His Spirit is power. He gives you the power to destroy every work of the devil and to destroy the works of your own flesh. He destroys every bondage. This is the reality of what your life can be! You can carry a yoke destroying anointing, so that you can walk completely free and see others set free by the power of God. You can't allow weakness to stop you. Understand though, that if you talk to God about power, He's going to talk to you about purity. You have to live a life of holiness, set apart unto Him, to carry His power.

Jesus said that all power and authority has been given unto Him (Matthew 28:18). If Jesus has all power, how much is left for the devil? Absolutely none. So, if you spend time talking about all of the things the devil is doing, you have to ask yourself how that's possible. Why is he being allowed to do anything when Jesus has all the power, and He lives in us? The only way to live defeated as a believer is to live in ignorance of the Word of God. Faith will be birthed in you when you allow the Holy Spirit to bring the Word of God alive. If you act on the seeds of faith that you receive, then the power of God *will* be activated in your life!

The second thing that comes into your life when the Holy Spirit fills you is love. I love everybody. I don't love everybody's ideas. I don't love everybody's doctrine. I don't agree with everybody's idea of who God is and what He's like. However, just because I don't love something someone believes or does, doesn't mean I don't love them. I know how to separate a person's ideas from the person themselves. God will give you the ability to love people that you wouldn't necessarily love on your own. He'll give you a heart to love and reach the lost with Gospel of Jesus Christ. He will give you the ability to love what God loves. An important thing to keep in mind, especially as God gives you a heart for the lost, is that you cannot act like the lost to try to see them saved. It actually disagrees with the gospel. You can stand against ideologies while loving people and standing for truth. The Gospel is the power of God unto salvation (Romans 1:16) and we have to stand boldly and unashamed and let the Gospel do its work!

The final thing that this verse says that God gives us is self-control or a sound mind. As you get filled with the Spirit and begin to walk in the fullness of His presence, He will destroy every yoke of mental and emotional instability. He will give you the ability to make sound decisions with precision and clarity of mind. These are just three of the things that will come when the Holy Spirit dwells in you! Always remember that nothing negative, whether it's fear, doubt, or instability, is from God. He has given you power, love, and a sound mind!

Now, let's discuss what the lasting evidence of the infilling of the Holy Spirit is. The Bible says in Acts 1:6-8,

'So, when they had come together, they asked Him, "Lord, will you at this time restore the kingdom to Israel?" He said to them, "It is not for you to know times or seasons that the Father has fixed by His own authority. But you will receive power when the Holy Spirit has come upon you, and you will be my witnesses in Jerusalem and in all Judea and Samaria, and to the end of the earth."'

The lasting evidence of the Holy Spirit in a person's life is *the power of God.* It's not the fact that they can speak in tongues or any gift that they receive. It is the power of God itself! Jesus told the disciples to wait in the city until they were *clothed with power from on high* (Luke 24:49). When you are filled with the Spirit, you become a conduit through which the power of God, the Holy Spirit, can flow to others. If God can get it through you, He will get it to you! God's desire is to make you the answer to someone else's prayers. When God answers their prayers through you, you will begin to see breakthrough like you've never known! Where you once found timidity, you will now find tenacity. Where you once found fear, you will now find love. Where you once found anxiety, you will now find authority, as the power of the Holy Spirit operates in your life!

Too many people have a *buffet Christianity* mentality. They want to pick and choose exactly what they want! They say strange things like, "God, I don't want the blessing, I want you." Where exactly is that kind of mentality in the Bible? When it comes to the working of the Holy Spirit, you don't have to decide between Him and His blessings. Without a doubt, we want God himself, but we can't separate God from who He is. God *is* a blesser. God *is* a giver. He wants to give good things to His children. The Bible says to "seek first the kingdom of God and His righteousness, and all these things will be added to you" (Matthew 6:33). The Bible clearly says that *all* these things will be added unto you. Many times, though, we act like it is humility to not receive something that God desires for us to have. We say, "Oh no, I don't need that." This is especially true with finances, however it's not wrong to have money and receive blessing from God. Money makes the world go round! We all have bills and responsibilities, and it is our Heavenly Father's desire to see His children blessed. Luke 12:32 says, "Fear not, little flock, for it is your Father's good pleasure to give you the kingdom." Is there anything lacking in the kingdom of God? No! He paves His streets with gold. We've allowed an ideology to seep in that says it's okay to have our needs met, but not to have an abundance. Receiving blessing has become a negative thing in some places, but it's not! God wants us to be blessed! He doesn't want us to be in lack. He wants us to have more than enough so that we can do the things that He's called us to do and bless other people. He's called us to take care of the poor. He's called us to love the widows. He's called us to take care of the orphans. You can't do that if you don't have the necessary resources! You have to understand that you can't live with a self-focused, "bless me" mentality. However, when you are seeking God's face, He will throw His hand, His blessing, in for free. If you think about it, no matter how hard you try, you can't get your hand very far from your face. If you find the hand of God, you're close. All you have to do is look up!

When God's power begins to move through somebody, sometimes people will get confused. Throughout the Bible, many people were mistaken as deity when God used them. Moses was called a god. Joseph appeared as a god in Egypt. Paul and Barnabas were mistaken as gods. When Paul was bitten by the viper, he shook it off unharmed! Initially the native people thought he was a criminal and justice had come, but when nothing happened to him, they completely changed their minds and decided he must have been a god (Acts 28:1-6)!

So, what do you do when God begins to use you to keep from becoming proud or taking credit for what He's doing? God gave Israel instruction in this area saying,

"Take care lest you forget the LORD your God by not keeping His commandments and His rules and His statutes, which I

command you today, lest, when you have eaten and are full and have built good houses and live in them, and when your herds and flocks multiply and your silver and gold is multiplied and all that you have is multiplied, then your heart be lifted up, and you forget the LORD your God, who brought you out of the land of Egypt, out of the house of slavery..." (Deuteronomy 8: 11-14).

I want to give you three very important things to remember as God begins to bless you and you walk in the power of His Spirit.

ALWAYS BE HUMBLE.

This is not a false humility like we talked about before. Humility is not thinking less of yourself but thinking of yourself less. It's not putting yourself down but simply making sure you are not always the center of your focus. One way to keep yourself humble is to keep the testimonies of God always before you. Hold a record in your heart of who God is and what He's done. By keeping the testimonies of God always before you, you will constantly remember what He did for Noah, Moses, Joseph, David, Abraham, Isaac, Jacob, the Prophets of Old, Peter, Paul, and John. We have a multitude of testimonies and a great cloud of witnesses that have gone before us! Don't even stop there. Continue to go through history and look at heroes of the faith closer to our time. Look at the lives of men like Billy Graham and Reinhard Bonnke. I even look at the lives of men of God around me today, like my Pastor Cleddie Keith. I hear the stories they tell and the testimonies of what they've seen God do and I say, "God, If you did it for them, you can do it for me." You see, the testimonies of God are the stories of Him doing great and mighty things for other people. This is the lens through which we need to see every challenge. There may be an obstacle in my way, but we know God never changes and He's going to see us through it. Victory is yours, right on the other side of this challenge! Too often what happens is that God will bring us through something, like a sickness or a financial attack, and we will almost immediately forget what He did. Revelation 19:10 says, "For the testimony of Jesus is the spirit of prophecy." When I hear a testimony and my faith is ignited, it becomes a prophecy and I know that God will do it again. It's important to read, listen, and meditate on those testimonies!

OBEY GOD'S WORD AND HIS VOICE.

Luke 10:38-42 says,

'As they traveled along, Jesus entered a village where a woman named Martha welcomed Him into her home. She had a sister named Mary, who sat at the Lord's feet listening to His message. But Martha was distracted by all the preparations to be made. She came to Jesus and said, "Lord, do You not care that my sister has left me to serve alone? Tell her to help me!" The Lord replied, "Martha, Martha, you are worried and upset about many things. But only one thing is necessary. Mary has chosen the good portion, and it will not be taken away from her."'

Here you see a picture of two different types of people when it comes to the word of God. One sat and listened to Jesus while the other was too distracted by the work. Yes, faith without works is dead, but you cannot perform the works at the cost of listening and obeying the voice of God. Don't get so caught up in the work that you forget the Lord of the work. You have to spend time in the word of God. You have to spend time in relationship with the living word—Jesus! You can't love Jesus and not love the Word of God, because they are One! This is the single biggest hinderance to victory in life. You only have one mountain to move, and that mountain is your ignorance to the word of God. If you move that mountain, God will remove every other mountain in your life for free.

Whatever your problem or struggle is today, ground yourself in God's Word and I guarantee you will see the victory! If you are not grounded in the word of God, then you will drift. It doesn't matter how much you pray. It doesn't matter how much time you say you spend in the presence of God. Your spiritual life will be evident by your words. When you are not grounded in the word of God, you become a two-legged negative, constantly rehearsing anything that has gone wrong or possibly could. By doing that, you prophesy negativity over yourself. We see an example of this in Jeremiah's day. The Bible tells us the people were saying the word of the Lord was a burden and Jeremiah told them they had perverted the word of God and become a prophecy unto themselves (Jeremiah 23:33-39). In other words, the burden they were experiencing was due to their own words, not the word of God. His Word is not and never has been a burden. Jesus said, "My yoke is easy, and My burden is light" (Matthew 11:30).

If you constantly see the negative, talk about yourself dying, speak of lack, or say how you can't overcome a situation, you are perverting the word of God and becoming a prophecy unto yourself. However, when you are grounded in the Word, there will be a flow of blessing like you've never seen. The Bible shows us how to overcome every obstacle. There is not a problem on this earth that the Bible does not have the answer to. Perpetual victory belongs to you. It just has to be enforced!

DIE TO YOURSELF.

The Holy Spirit gives you power to overcome all the works of the flesh. I know people who constantly struggle with the flesh. They want to serve God, but they are constantly giving into the flesh, taking two steps forward and then three steps back. Life doesn't have to be that way! You can be an overcomer. You can see all of the works of the flesh be destroyed. God gives us that power when the Holy Spirit comes upon us!

Romans 8:3-11 says,

"For God has done what the law, weakened by the flesh, could not do. By sending His own Son in the likeness of sinful flesh and for sin, He condemned sin in the flesh, in order that the righteous requirement of the law might be fulfilled in us, who walk not according to the flesh but according to the Spirit. For those who live according to the flesh set their minds on the things of the flesh, but those who live according to the Spirit set their minds on the things of the Spirit. For to set the mind on the flesh is death, but to set the mind on the Spirit is life and peace. For the mind that is set on the flesh is hostile to God, for it does not submit to God's law; indeed, it cannot. Those who are in the flesh cannot please God. You, however, are not in the flesh but in the Spirit, if in fact the Spirit of God dwells in you. Anyone who does not have the Spirit of Christ does not belong to Him. But if Christ is in you, although the body is dead because of sin, the Spirit is life because of righteousness. If the Spirit of Him who raised Jesus from the dead dwells in you, He who raised Christ Jesus from the dead will also give life to your mortal bodies through His Spirit who dwells in you."

You can destroy every work of the flesh in your life. You never have to go give into sin a single day in your life. You cannot blame the devil for your works of the flesh, as a child of God. It is your responsibility by the grace of God to cast off the works of the flesh and walk in the victory He purchased for you!

1 John 5:18 says,

"We know that everyone who has been born of God does not keep on sinning, but He who was born of God protects him, and the evil one does not touch him."

We know that everyone born of God does not keep on sinning. Get that into your spirit. You cannot live as a child of God and live in sin. The wages of sin is ultimately death (Romans 6:23) and unfortunately it leaves a path of destruction behind it. If you are living in sin, you have separated yourself from the only One who can help you overcome it. Sin will always stop the flow of the Holy Spirit in your life! You have to die to self and live a righteous life. You will see the Holy Spirit bring victory in every area and live completely and totally free!

the IMPARTATION of the PRESENCE of GOD

Now, as we've talked about previously, God's presence *is* His Holy Spirit. When the presence of God fills a place or a person, it's the Holy Spirit that come. Whenever someone has an encounter with God's presence, they have a choice. They can choose to walk away from Him entirely, or walk in the fullness that He has for them. The gifts and callings of God are without repentance (Romans 11:29). God can give you something that you never develop or learn to walk in, and you can live totally miserably. On the other hand, God can impart His presence to you, and you can choose to walk in the lasting evidence of that impartation, the power of God, day in and day out.

No matter what, you have to have to have an appetite for the presence of God. You should have a desire for God that surpasses my desire for Skyline Chili when I see the sign. Are you hungry for God? You can tell what you're hungry for by what you crave. What do you spend your time thinking about and pursing? You should have a passion for God's presence and the things He's given you to do. If you're a pastor and all you talk about is sports, then it may be that you shouldn't be a pastor. Your appetite is for sports! Now, there's nothing wrong with having a passion for sports or business or whatever it may be unless it's drawing you away from God. God just wants our passion and attention! He wants to take people and fill them with His presence and then put them in every arena of society, and that includes everything from sports to construction to politics. He'll fill you and use you in whatever field He places you. You just have to know what He's called you to do! The greatest failure in life is to be successful at the wrong assignment. You may have great success in a particular area, but if it's not what you're called to, you'll be miserable. You may appear to have everything together, but it's a failure, if it's not what God made you for.

You need to ask yourself: What do I have an appetite for? What is my passion? Sadly, many people, church people, just go through the motions. They're saved, love God, and are on their way to heaven. However, they live with no passion. They just live day by day and go to church on the weekends and live a life devoid of passion. If you're doing what God created you to do, life won't be that way. You should live with passion!

2 Timothy 3:1-5 says:

"But understand this, that in the last days there will come times of difficulty. For people will be lovers of self, lovers of money, proud, arrogant, abusive, disobedient to their parents, ungrateful, unholy, heartless, unappeasable, slanderous, without self-control, brutal, not loving good, treacherous, reckless, swollen with conceit, lovers of pleasure rather than lovers of God, having the appearance of godliness, but denying its power. Avoid such people."

Let's look at this verse a bit. It says there will come *times of difficulty.* Remember, faith does not deny reality. There will be challenges, but it's not the same for the believer as it is for people without God. Christians *face* difficulties, but sinners *have* difficulties. There's a big difference there! A sinner doesn't have the promises of God's word when they face challenges. The Bible is a book of covenant and unless you are walking with God, you can't stand on the promises that it carries. However, we face trials with His presence and every promise of His Word. When a Christian comes into a challenge, we come with guaranteed victory, knowing that we will see every wall that stands before us come crumbling down.

The verse above gives quite an extensive list of the types of people we will encounter in the world—lovers of all kinds of evil. It says they will *have the appearance of godliness but deny its power.* Listen, the Spirit and the Word of God always agree. People who have an *appearance* of godliness, but deny its power, which is the working of the Holy Spirit, will always be very argumentative. They have to rely on arguments because they have no demonstration. Without the power of God, churches have to rely on programs, technology, and all sorts of things to keep people entertained. There should be evidence of the impartation of God's presence! Without it, you will have to fill the void with all kinds of things. Jesus addressed this with the religious people of His day saying,

"Woe to you, scribes and Pharisees, hypocrites! For you are like whitewashed tombs, which outwardly appear beautiful, but within are full of dead people's bones and all uncleanness. So, you also outwardly appear righteous to others, but within you are full of hypocrisy and lawlessness" (Matthew 23:27-28)

They looked great on the outside—ornate, impressive, and religious—but there was no substance to their religion. They were filthy, dead, and empty on the inside. They had the *appearance of godliness* but denied its power. They weren't even able to recognize the very Messiah they'd been waiting for!

Religious people are uncomfortable with the presence of God. Our oldest daughter experienced this once with someone she invited to a service at our church. The presence of God moved in a powerful way, but the moment they walked out, the argument began. He didn't have questions or anything positive to say about what had happened. He was full of arguments about what had happened because he had all Word and no Spirit!

When people don't have experience with God, all they have is an argument! Now it's important to understand that many people start here, and there's nothing wrong with that. My six-year-old has never seen the Star Wars movies, but he knows a lot about it. He knows more about them than my wife who's seen the movies! All he knows are the things he's been told, but he's passionate about it. If someone questions something that he says or believes about Star Wars, he *will* argue about it, not disrespectfully, but passionately. My point is that there are times when we truly believe the Bible with childlike faith, even if we haven't experienced it. As children's pastors, we saw this often. Children can receive information and believe it wholeheartedly. You would not believe the way that a child will argue for something if they believe it's right and true. They will argue it tooth and nail! However, this belief is often without experience. They haven't actually experienced that which they're believing and receiving, which is okay, because they're children! That's a great place to start, but a terrible place to end. God doesn't want us to just know about Him, but to experience what His Word says we can! This is why it's so important to learn from those who have gone before us. We always have to be teachable and willing to hear from those who have more wisdom and experience than we do. We have to allow people that have gone before us to come along and help us in situations that we haven't walked through before. There is nothing wrong with those children receiving what they're taught and believing it without having experienced it yet! They're young. They're learning from people who have seen more than they have. Now, you could still have faith only from believing and reading what the word of God says. However, if you can have someone come alongside you and help you activate that faith by their experience, then you are in a whole new realm. At that point, you've read it, believed it, and now you've heard a testimony of how it could be applied to your life through the power of a testimony! Healing is a great example. We can read about healing in the Bible and know in our heads that Jesus healed people. We can believe that the disciples and the apostles healed people. All throughout the Scripture, we see healing and know God can do it. However, it's totally different to hear someone say, "let me tell you about how Jesus healed *me*." Having the basis of faith in the word of God is important. You have to have a foundation of faith that can be activated, but it has to beyond the realm of head knowledge to experience and encounter!

If there is no working of the Spirit of God in your life, you may have the fruit of faith, but you won't have gift of faith that operates by the Holy Spirit. You may have received enough faith to believe God to be saved, but then you stopped, content to live dry and devoid of God's presence and power. After you are saved and receive the fruit of that faith, you have to step into the demonstration and power of God by the working of the Holy Spirit. Faith is an active thing! It will give you the boldness and tenacity to step out into what you're called to do, operating in the power of God.

Now, there are two different ways that the Spirit of God is imparted in Scripture. The first is by the laying on of hands, which we see many times. In Acts 8, we see an example of this in Phillip's ministry. Philip was an evangelist. In this story, He was in Samaria having great success and seeing multitudes converted as He preached the gospel. However, there was more.

Acts 8:14-17 says,

> *"Now when the apostles at Jerusalem heard that Samaria had received the word of God, they sent to them Peter and John, who came down and prayed for them that they might receive the Holy Spirit, for He had not yet fallen on any of them, but they had only been baptized in the name of the Lord Jesus. Then they laid their hands on them and they received the Holy Spirit."*

Philip was preaching salvation and seeing success, but those believers hadn't yet received the fullness of what God wanted for them. The Holy Spirit was imparted to the new believers by the laying on of the apostles' hands. We see this again in Scripture after Saul had His encounter with Jesus on the road to Damascus. He had been blinded and had gone without food and water for 3 days. Acts 9:17-18 says,

> *'So, Ananias departed and entered the house. And laying his hands on him he said, "Brother Saul, the Lord Jesus who appeared to you on the road by which you came has sent me so that you may regain your sight and be filled with the Holy Spirit." And immediately something like scales fell from his eyes, and he regained his sight.'*

His sight was restored, and he received the Holy Spirit *by the laying on of Ananias' hands*. So, we see that one of the ways that the presence of the God, the Holy Spirit, is imparted is through someone who already has it laying their hands on you. This doesn't mean you receive *their* Holy Spirit. You receive *the* Holy Spirit. There is not one Holy Spirit for new believers and one for mature believers. There's not one Holy Spirit for adults, one for youth, and one for children. There is *one* Holy Spirit. One size fits all! A child could have the same amount of anointing as an adult, because God is no respecter of persons (Acts 10:34).

The other way that we see the presence of God can be imparted is by the prayer of faith. This could be a couple of different ways. There are times in large crowds of people that the Holy Spirit may begin to move, and an impartation comes upon one section of the crowd as someone prays. They may not have to lay hands on every single person, but as they pray, the Holy Spirit comes. That's the prayer of faith going forth and causing an impartation of His presence! Another way we see this is an individual becoming so desperate in their prayer for impartation that they receive without anyone laying hands on them at all. This wouldn't be someone begging God, but a person asking in faith to receive the promise according to the word of God. God isn't moved by need or begging; He is moved by faith!

When the Holy Spirit is imparted into your life, you have access to all the gifts and the fruits that come with Him. Every gift that the Holy Spirit carries is imparted into you. There are many people that operate in the fruits of the spirit, without operating in the gifts of the spirit. Learning to walk in the Holy Spirit is not a one-time thing. You have to learn to abide in Him, as a lifestyle!

It's not enough to have one encounter with God that you're still talking about two months later if you haven't received anything from Him since then. You can live in such a way that you encounter the very presence of God on a daily basis. The Bible says that faith without works is dead (James 2:14), but we don't live in such a way that we're trying to get a certain amount of works accomplished to meet some sort of requirement. It's about knowing what God has said and putting it into action to fulfill that which He called you to do. James 2:17-18 says,

> 'So also, faith by itself if it does not have works, is dead.
> But someone will say, "You have faith and I have works."
> Show me your faith apart from your works,
> and I will show you my faith by my works.'

We are saved by grace through faith, but once we're saved, we get to work! Pray like it all depends on God and work like it all depends on you. Listen, you'll know if you have an impartation from God. An encounter with His presence always changes you, from the inside out. Understand though that God doesn't make robots. When you encounter His presence, you will still have all of the things that make you who you are, but you will be *changed* for the better.

I love to tell the story of a young man that we know who was picked up off of the streets, an absolute mess. He was put into a faith-based program, that included rehab, but was really about life rehabilitation, by the power of the Holy Spirit. This young man was radically transformed! After a period of time, he went back to the community he came from, and he saw someone he used to know. They actually came up to him and asked him if he was related to himself. The person was shocked when he told them that he *was* that man. This was a person that knew him before he encountered God but didn't recognize him! He was so radically transformed that they could see that he *resembled* the man he used to be, but he wasn't him anymore.

Now, I want to tell you a story from my own life. When we first got married, my wife had significant health issues. One day, God spoke to me that if I would take her to this particular church where God was moving, He would heal her. That was all I needed to hear. This church was in the midst of a major revival that had been going on for quite a few years. They were having services nightly and a couple times a week, they would have morning services as well. The very first night we were there, a word of knowledge was given, and my wife was healed of a major birth defect! The next day, we came back to another service and the pastor's daughter was leading the service. At that time, I had some theological concerns about women in leadership that I no longer have, but I was open enough to receive anything that God wanted me to have. I want to tell you that you will never enjoy the fruits of any doctrine that you choose to stand against! So, this conflict was going on in me while the pastor's daughter was leading the service. I honestly can't tell you anything she preached! At the end, she made an altar call and I just sat down on the front row. She was moving through the crowd, praying for people. She prayed for one particular woman who fell out under the power of God, at my feet. The woman began to wail. Now, I don't know if you've ever heard somebody wail, but you would know if you had. I'd heard people cry. I'd heard people weep. This, though, was the first time I had ever heard someone wailing. Now, because of the great mercy that I have, I began to pray for her, and this is what I said: "Oh God, please shut this woman up." I'm just being honest! Her wailing was absolutely ear-piercing. Well, God didn't answer my prayer, so I got up and went back to my seat.

I was sitting back at my seat with all kinds of issues. I wasn't even sure I was okay with women preaching and then there was a woman wailing so loud, I needed earplugs. My wife came to me after getting prayed for and asked me if I wanted to go up for prayer. I was thinking, "Did you not hear that woman up front wailing? Did you miss that?" At that moment, I had a decision to make. I had to decide whether I would allow internal conflicts to keep me from receiving a blessing. I had to decide if I would allow the piercing cries of a wailing woman to keep me from receiving from God. After a moment, I enthusiastically told my wife, "Well, it can't hurt anything." We walked to the front and the woman came toward me smiling and said, "What can I pray for you?" In that moment, the entire scene changed. I was no longer in that building, but in my heart, I was standing in the throne room of God. The Father was sitting on the throne, and I was standing before Him. Jesus came and stood beside me, as if to say, "it's okay." It was like the Father was asking me, "What do you want?" Without hesitation, the only thing that would come out of my mouth, the only prayer that I had was a loud cry of desperation: "God, I want to know you in the fullness of your love!" In the natural, all that happened was I calmly said to the woman was, "I want to know God in the fullness of His love." She smiled kindly and said, "I can pray for that." She prayed for me and absolutely nothing happened. I didn't fall out under the power of God. There were no fireworks or goosebumps. I didn't feel a single thing.

Shortly after that, we left the revival and went home. At that time, my in-laws had a barn that my father-in-law used to run his business from. They lived about five minutes away from us so I would go over early in the morning before work and use that space to pray. Morning by morning I would go. Then one morning, as I was praying, God moved and absolutely shook me took my core.

His presence was so powerful and so real that I actually opened up the door and looked outside because I thought someone was there. However, it was the Holy Spirit bringing an impartation. It was the answer to the prayer that I had prayed, and the release of the deposit I'd received by the laying on of hands in that service. My wife and I went to this service at the instruction of God so that my wife could receive a harvest, and she did. She received her healing! However, what I didn't realize at that time is that when you reap a harvest, there's always seed. In that revival, I received a seed and from that moment, God began to give me the impartation I desired, which was to know Him, in the fullness of His love.

Sometime later, my wife told me what happened that morning from her perspective. After that encounter with God in the barn, I went home, got ready for work, and told my wife goodbye for the day. As soon as I left, she prayed, "God, that's my husband, but that's not my husband. What has happened to him?" I tell you that whole story to tell you that when you really encounter God, there will inevitably be a change. Impartation will *always* change you.

Paul told Timothy,

"I thank God whom I serve, as did my ancestors, with a clear conscience, as I remember you constantly in my prayers night and day. As I remember your tears, I long to see you, that I may be filled with joy. I am reminded of your sincere faith, a faith that dwelt first in your grandmother Lois and your mother Eunice and now, I am sure, dwells in you as well. For this reason, I remind you to fan into flame the gift of God, which is in you through the laying on of my hands, for God gave us a spirit not of fear but of power and love and self-control" (2 Timothy 1:3-7)

There is an impartation from generation to generation! That doesn't necessarily have to be through blood relation. The Bible talks about there being an impartation of three to four generations of those who do wicked. That doesn't mean that it comes through your bloodline, but just that if you do wickedness, you carry the consequences of three to four generations of wickedness. *However,* if you do righteous, you don't just reap the blessing of three to four generations of righteousness, but the blessings of thousands of generations (Deuteronomy 5:10).

Another thing that we receive by impartation is faith! We see that in regards to Timothy in the verse above. Without faith, it is impossible to please God (Hebrews 11:6). If you don't value impartation, both the Giver and the gifts that He gives, then anything imparted to you will remain dormant in your life. It will never be activated and you and the generations after you will live in bondage. You have to place a value on the impartation of the presence of God. You have to desire the things that God gives! Paul said to "earnestly desire the greater spiritual gifts" (1 Corinthians 14:1). These things come through impartation, so you have to desire the impartation of the presence of God in order to receive. You have to hunger for the presence of God to come and dwell on the side of you. This is not a one-time thing, but a continuous, life-long pursuit of that which you were made for!

If you are not saved, you need to understand that encountering God's presence will actually do you more harm than good if you experience an impartation and choose to walk away. However, you are just one prayer away from salvation! If you don't know Jesus, I invite you to pray this prayer out loud:

"Dear Lord Jesus, I ask You now to come into my heart and forgive me of all my sin. I believe You are the Son of God and

that You died on a cross for me. I believe that You are risen from the dead and that You're coming back again, for me. I ask You to wash me and cleanse me! Set me free from every bondage of sin and my past choices. Thank You that You love me and have adopted me into Your family. I ask You to fill me with Your promised Holy Spirit! I ask You to give me a hunger for the things of God. Thank You that I am saved. Thank You that I'm a new creation. I will serve You all the days of my life, from this day forward."

If you prayed that prayer, you just stepped from death into life, from bondage into freedom, and from the world into the family of God. Whether you just got saved or you've been saved for many years, we *must* desire impartation. It's equally as important once we receive that impartation to protect it. If you plant a seed, you don't expect to receive a harvest the next day. That doesn't mean that there aren't times that God does miraculous things like that. However, in general, seeds have to be cultivated and that is our responsibility. Once a seed has been imparted in our heart, we have to feed it with the word. We have to spend time in His presence. We have to foster an environment that it can grow in and then you watch it flourish. When we do, we'll see it impact other areas in your heart and reap a harvest. When I came back with that seed from the revival service, I wasn't different overnight, but over time, it was clear that I had been changed! God wants to impart His presence to you, and He can touch you right where you are. I encourage you to pray these words out loud:

"Holy Spirit, I welcome Your presence. I want to encounter Your presence like I never have before. I welcome You to flood this room, my home, and my whole life. Holy Spirit, I ask You to

impart to me all the fruits and gifts that You carry. I ask You to show me what You want me to see. I ask you to pour the love of the Father into my heart, as Your Word says. Plant seeds of truth in my heart, that I will never be the same again. I welcome You, Holy Spirit. Come and change my life for the better, in Jesus' name!"

CONCLUSION

As the presence of God becomes your way of life, everything will change. All of your regrets will dissolve. All of your shame, fear, anger, and condemnation will melt away. As the presence of God becomes like liquid love in your life, all the things that hindered freedom will begin to fade away. The presence of God is tangible and transferrable, and it will change everything if you choose to fully embrace Him. You can live a lifestyle of the presence of God and it's not complicated. As a matter of fact, it is so simple. Every day when you wake up, just say, "Welcome, Holy Spirit." As you say that, with a pure heart, the presence of God will fill you. It is that simple. Even as I write this, I can feel the presence of God answer that request in my life and it will be the same for you.

The presence of God will help you fully understand what it means to be a new creation in God. *All* of the old has passed away and *all* things become new! The presence of God will make you understand what it means to be seated in heavenly places in Christ Jesus. You are not fighting *for* a place of victory, but in the presence of God you are already seated *in* a place of victory. There is no war being waged in the presence of God. The war has already been won and you are in a place of perfect peace. There may be a war raging all around you, but in the presence of God, you are safe. You don't have to fight anymore. The only fight you have to fight is the good fight of faith!

Always remember that the presence of God will bring understanding to the word of God. You need the presence of God *and* His word. As the old saying goes:

All Word and no Spirit, you dry up.
All Spirit and no Word, you blow up.
With the Spirit and the Word, you grow up.

When the Spirit and the Word agree in your life, the mountains will begin to be removed. The only mountain you have to move is the mountain of ignorance of the word of God. If you will seek God in His Word and allow His presence to remove that mountain, every other mountain will be moved for free. All you have to do is speak to them to move and they will go. As Psalm 97:5 says, "The mountains melt like wax before the LORD, before the Lord of all the earth."

At the beginning of this book, we talked about Obed-Edom's family, who received a blessing from God's presence and then gave it all to seek after Him. I hope that after reading this book you are hungrier for God's presence than you've ever been before. Just as the presence of God became everything to Obed-Edom's household, we have to come to the point that it's everything to us. Right now, welcome the Holy Spirit. Tell Him that He can have all of you. Empty yourself to receive everything He has for you. Make the decision to be all in because I promise you, the reward far outweighs any upfront costs. Wherever you are right now, choose to follow the road that leads to peace. You can come without fear and trust Him to guide you to exactly where you need to be. There is no better place to be than in the will of God, right in the center of His presence. It doesn't matter if you never leave your small town or you're in a different city or nation from one week to the next. Wherever you are will be home, if you live a life in pursuit of the presence of God!

ENDNOTES

1. Tseng, J., Poppenk, J. Brain meta-state transitions demarcate thoughts across task contexts exposing the mental noise of trait neuroticism. *Nat Commun* 11, 3480 (2020). https://doi.org/10.1038/s41467-020-17255-9

ABOUT THE AUTHOR

AARON and JULIE SCHILLING have been in passionate pursuit of God's presence for many years. Seeking His presence has been a lifelong journey that has only gotten better with time. They have been married for over 24 years and reside on land that has been in the family since the 1800s, in the greater Cincinnati, OH area. They currently lead & operate Life Together Ministry.